THE DON'T SWEAT GUIDE
TO HOLIDAYS

THE DON'T SWEAT GUIDE
TO HOLIDAYS

Enjoying the Festivities and
Letting Go of the Tension

By the Editors of Don't Sweat Press
Foreword by Richard Carlson, Ph.D.

New York

Hyperion books are available for special promotions and premiums.
For details contact Michael Rentas, Manager, Inventory and Premium Sales,
Hyperion, 77 West 66th Street, 11th floor, New York, New York 10023,
or call 212-456-0133.

ISBN: 0-7868-8891-1

FIRST EDITION

10 9 8 7 6 5 4 3 2 1

Contents

Foreword

To many, the holidays represent the best of times and the worst of times. They are both joyful and at the same time stressful. It's a strange thing. We love our family and friends more than just about anyone, but somehow, our interaction with them causes us the most distress—particularly during the holidays.

Even the media emphasizes the stress somehow created by the holidays. Sure, it mentions the joys—particularly the superficial parts, such as shopping—but there is a lot of emphasis on the loneliness and emptiness, as well. The advertisers would like us to believe that if we just would buy and receive the right gifts—and bump up our credit card bills—all will be fine. Deep down, however, we know that's not the answer.

The editors of Don't Sweat Press have done a stellar job at explaining this strange dynamic, and more importantly, they have created effective strategies to deal with it. They explain, in easy-to-understand and simple ways, how to deal with the stress that we usually associate with the holidays.

This book covers everything from finding ways to simplify the holidays, to saving time and money, increasing creativity, and making the entire season more satisfying. It will help you anticipate the holidays in a more positive light, making the best of each and every day along the way, and creating better memories. It will help you remember the true meaning of what the holidays are about—God, family, giving, and love. It will remind you of the gift of service, of helping those in need. And in my opinion, the wisdom of this message will spread through your life during the rest of the year.

One thing is certain. Like clockwork, the holidays will be here every single year of your life, whether you want them to be or not. There's no escaping them. They can be stressful, miserable and overwhelming—or they can be fun, filled with laughter, and something you look forward to. This book can point you in the direction of making the holidays the priceless gift that God intended them to be; a celebration. I wish you a happy holiday season, as well as a happy rest of the year. I'm convinced that anyone reading this book will have one of the best holidays ever!

Richard Carlson
Benicia, California, April 2003

THE DON'T SWEAT GUIDE
TO HOLIDAYS

1.

Plan the Best
Holidays for You

Holidays are the highlights of our lives. Many of our most cherished memories are wrapped around holiday celebrations. Much of what we envision for the future is tied to holidays. Some of our most far-reaching charitable work is inspired by them. These special occasions are parties, reunions, incentives, and yardsticks, all wrapped in the same package.

Certain holidays commemorate the departed, while others focus more specifically on the lives and accomplishments of visionaries. We remember the heroes of the battlefield on Veterans Day and the heroes of industry on Labor Day. We honor our country (Independence Day, Flag Day) and our environment (Earth Day, Arbor Day). These are just our secular holidays. When you add religious observances and festivals, you have a calendar packed so full of tributes and special events that if you're of a mind, you can celebrate virtually nonstop.

Along with this attention to celebration comes the pressure to make every holiday a winner. Our sense of urgency is intensified by TV and movies, which beguile us with unrealistic holiday models— fantasy families enjoying fantasy celebrations. At work, our colleagues routinely inquire, "What are you doing for the holiday?" as if it were a given that we would be planning something extraordinary. Too often, we convert these external cues to internal pressure to create memorable events. If we can't measure up to our outsized expectations, our holidays become disappointments rather than sources of satisfaction.

You can avoid holiday pressure by establishing your own agenda for each of these special days. Don't try to fashion your holidays after the fairy tales that the mass media concocts. You have a real-world agenda that will point you in the right direction. If friends ask what you're planning for the holiday, don't be embarrassed or reluctant to respond, "Nothing in particular." Planning what is right and best for you is what makes the holiday special.

2.

The "4-P" Approach
to Happy Holidays

Holidays are deceptively demanding. We think of them as a respite, as time off, but are they really that? Think about the roster of holidays that most of us observe—Martin Luther King Jr. Day, Presidents' Day, Easter/Passover, Mother's Day, Memorial Day, Father's Day, Independence Day, Labor Day, Halloween, Veterans Day, Thanksgiving, Christmas/Hanukkah, and New Year's. Celebrate each of these holidays as the months roll along, and you could be involved in nearly year-round planning—and worrying about the outcome. Daunting as this list seems, it's probably shorter than your actual lineup.

If you treat these occasions seriously—that is, you work diligently to put together the best affairs for your family and friends—you won't find much time to have fun. In fact, anxiety and tension can accompany most holidays more than any enjoyment or satisfaction. To help assure that your holidays are joyous, consider the "4-P" approach.

Prioritize. Decide which holidays you want to emphasize, and then focus most of your attention there. Also, prioritize your goals for your key holidays. For those holidays that are low on your priority list, go with the flow—and don't take on more than you can handle comfortably.

Plan. Map out the ideal holiday for you. Determine what elements you'll need, how much they'll cost, and what resources— financial and human—you can bring to bear. Develop a task list and an implementation schedule for your party plan.

Publicize. Your plan may seem perfect to you, but if it isn't equally amenable to the folks with whom you'll be sharing your holidays, it could generate frustration rather than enthusiasm. Think of your plan as a proposal that must be reviewed and critiqued by all involved. You're accustomed to doing this at the office, where consensus often is critical, but it's just as essential on the home front. Once you collect feedback, revise your plan to reflect the new input.

Party. When you've established your holiday priorities, developed a preliminary plan, publicized your blueprint among key audiences, and modified it according to their suggestions, you're ready to cut loose and enjoy yourself. This final "P" is every bit as important as the other three, since more enjoyable holidays for you is the ultimate objective.

3.

Whose True Meaning?

If you watch television news as a major holiday approaches, you're likely to hear a commentator lament about the commercialization of holidays and encourage us to get back to the "true meaning" of the event ahead. It seems a noble, even sobering thought, suggesting as it does that we've been squandering our energy on something less than the true meaning of the holiday. However, this pronouncement won't hold up to close scrutiny. We might well ask this pundit, "Whose true meaning are you talking about?" In our melting pot of a society, holidays mean many things to many people.

To some, holidays are principally religious occasions—special opportunities for worship, contemplation, or even repentance. For these people, the decorations, feasts, and other customs associated with holidays may have secondary meaning only.

For others, holidays mean family—chances to gather with loved ones who may never get together except on these occasions. Nothing else about holidays is as important as assembling the family.

Kids, with their limited experience, may have a narrower perspective about holidays. For them, holidays mean gifts—and they're not likely to broaden their outlook for some time. No use lecturing the littlest ones about the true meaning of the holidays. Each time they open a package and find a shiny toy inside, their understanding of the holiday's true meaning is reinforced.

Retailers may have yet another take on holidays. Whatever their personal beliefs, their businesses sometimes depend on seasonal sales, so for them, holidays mean unusually hard work—and considerable anguish or joy over the results.

With so many different approaches—each as legitimate as the next—it is important to respect the beliefs and customs of others. Perhaps we ought to consider the practice of mutual respect as the true meaning of holidays. With that as our starting point, it would be hard for us to go wrong.

4.

Getting Ready

Preparing for a holiday can be simple or demanding, depending on what's expected of you and what you expect of yourself. For example, once your children have grown, your Halloween preparations may involve little more than purchasing a few bags of candy to dispense to the neighborhood goblins and ghouls.

On the other hand, Christmas preparation can be monumental—select, set up, and trim the tree; decorate the house and yard; write and mail the cards; purchase and wrap the gifts. If you're hosting the Christmas gathering, getting ready becomes an even more arduous and time-consuming process.

That's why preparing for a major holiday celebration should begin with establishing a state of mental readiness. Of course, your preparations will involve a list of holiday chores, but as a veteran holiday manager, you're used to ticking items off a lengthy to-do list.

Mentally preparing for a holiday means developing just the right balance of idealism and realism. Ideally, you accomplish all your holiday chores with time left over for relaxation. Realistically, you know that you may not get everything done, so budget some time for relaxation now. Ideally, everyone will be thrilled with every gift. Realistically, some gifts will be the wrong size or the wrong color, so resolve to stay calm when gifts go awry. Ideally, your guests will hungrily devour all the food you prepare. Realistically, someone won't eat the pumpkin pie, so pledge to keep cool—and recycle what you can for leftovers.

Finding your equilibrium is so important to a successful holiday that you might consider holding off on your chores until you reach that state of readiness. When your mindset is right, you'll find that just about everything goes well—and you'll remain poised and effective when things don't.

5.

Set Your Holiday Agenda

Holidays are upon us before we know it, sometimes leaving us in a state of panic that becomes a self-fulfilling prophecy. We're so afraid that we won't get everything done that our constant worrying prevents us from getting everything done. However, holidays can be within your control. Not only can you get every task finished, but efficiency will allow you to relax and enjoy each holiday to its fullest.

The key is to develop a good game plan along with a workable timeline. Everyone's holiday hit list will differ, of course, but here are some major categories for your schedule.

Identify and resolve major issues. Who will host this year's celebration? What time will it take place? Will it occur on the holiday itself, or will you need to observe the holiday a day or two early or late to accommodate everyone's schedule? Will any participants need help with travel? Once you have these important issues resolved, the rest of your planning will fall into place. Figure to have everything set in this category at least one month in advance.

Prepare a holiday budget. It needn't be formal, but try to rough out a holiday spending plan. Include any costs for travel, groceries, gifts, and decorations. When you know what you can afford to spend, you'll be surprised how easy it is to spend just that amount.

Write and mail your cards. Plan to have everything mailed two weeks before the holiday. That will give you time to amend any oversights and handle late additions to your holiday list.

Purchase and wrap your gifts. Plan to have all your gifts purchased two weeks before the holiday. Then if you encounter a snafu with a catalog or e-mail order, you have some time to sort it out. When you finish early, you'll need a secure place to store your presents where curious people won't find them!

Decorate. If you've completed your other action items, you can save decorating until near the end. Now you have the opportunity to get really creative rather than throwing things together under the pressure of time.

Your last item should be to relax. You've done it all—and with enough time left over to help out any less efficient friends or family. Happy holiday!

6.

The Card Competition

Our tradition of exchanging holiday cards has evolved over the years—but it isn't clear if all of the changes have been positive. Cards began pretty simply as a way of expressing holiday wishes to a handful of friends and family. Some early cards boasted a few well-chosen manufactured elements, but the packaging tended to be secondary. Our brief, personalized messages were the most important components.

Over the years, cards have become more ornate—to say nothing of more expensive. Many include commercially produced verse along with lavish seasonal art. We often augment these store-bought effects with lengthy personal letters detailing family developments during the past year along with photographs of kids and pets. What began as a simple custom has become a full-blown production number.

Even more significant have been the changes in our card lists. Maintaining a card list used to be an uncomplicated affair. Now, it's a time-consuming, year-round project that involves updating dozens of names that span our personal and professional lives. We're determined to send a card to each person on our list each year. If the unthinkable happens—someone that we overlooked or never even considered sends us a card—we hurriedly send a card to our new holiday pal and expand our card list once more.

The intensity we bring to greeting cards has a downside—the worry and anxiety it causes. A healthier approach may be to maintain a reasonably sized card list, prepare a message that doesn't tax your emotional reserves, mail your cards punctually, and then relax and take pleasure in a job well done.

Once it's finished, let it be finished. If you get a card from someone not on your list, it's okay. A friend wanted to remember you on the holiday; that's a nice thing, not a call for reciprocity. You can add that person to next year's list or even give your friend a call. That will enhance your holiday without extending the card competition.

7.

A Sensible Card List

You can avoid the dizzying competition that holiday greeting card exchanges can generate by getting a good head start on the project. Think of it as a year-round endeavor rather than a last-minute rush job that finds you in a long line at the post office just before the holiday.

Your first task, of course, is your card list. You have a ready-made nucleus of your family, close friends, and colleagues. If maintaining your list is an ongoing task, you'll be able to update it without much trouble and expand it at your leisure. Once you allow enough time for the task, it won't matter whether you're sending ten cards or a hundred. You'll have plenty of time to complete the job without stress.

Perhaps a more complicated task is deciding which names to add to your list and which to drop. Adding to your list can become laborious if you intend to practice what might be thought of as "blanket reciprocity"—a determination to send a card to everyone who sends one to you. While this seems like an honorable intention, it can break down in practice when you find that you're sending cards to your car dealer, your insurance agent, and even your elected officials, only because you received cards from them.

If you get one of these "greetings," are you obliged to reciprocate? You have no more responsibility there than you do for sending cards in the first place. Cards are a voluntary expression of your best wishes. Send them to the people you most want to reach, and don't worry about reciprocity.

Take the same approach to pruning your list. It doesn't matter how recently you may have seen someone on your list. If you want to be remembered, and to show long-lost friends that you remember them, keep sending them cards. With a few well-chosen words, your greeting will be anything but superficial, and well worth the price of postage.

8.

It's Okay If You
Can't Bake This Year

Are you one of those wonderful folks who puts the sparkle in the holidays with your delicious baked goods? Perhaps it's those special cookies that you turn out, dozen upon dozen on racks stacked perilously throughout your kitchen. Or maybe it's your signature bread, each year with a different nut or fruit filling to surprise everyone.

You're the key player in an unforgettable holiday tradition—but what happens on that one holiday when you can't bake? Perhaps the demands on your time are too great, or you can't afford to purchase all the supplies, or, for whatever reason, you're simply not up to the task. You may be disappointed, but don't let this be a source of undue stress.

The one thing that we can be sure of is that our circumstances will change. Change may be mild or dramatic, but it's inevitable. Cutting back on your holidays may be an appropriate way of responding to change. It doesn't mean that your holiday pleasure must suffer.

Get creative in coping with change. If time is the issue, you might prevail upon a family member or friend to help you gather ingredients, wash and dry the dishes, or wrap and distribute the gifts. This can be a great way to extend and expand your baking tradition to make it even more inclusive.

However, if you find that you can't bake this year, that's okay. Don't spend too much time worrying that you'll disappoint your list of pastry recipients. It's true that the people who expected and relished their holiday goodies will miss them, but it's just as true that they'll go on to enjoy this holiday, even if it doesn't include the usual tin of treats from you. Like you, they'll recognize that things change, and they'll understand if you can't bake.

9.

Who Hosts?

Some holidays are marred or even ruined by disagreements within the family about who will host the celebration. In many families, the host earns that role almost by common consent; it's been happening that way for so many years that everyone just assumes the tradition will continue. However, over the years, needs and circumstances change. It's important to address those changes to keep the hosting question from spoiling your holidays.

For example, the year may have meant relocation for one or more family members who now are some distance from the home of the traditional host. Perhaps a switch to a more central location for the holiday gathering would work better for these participants.

Because of illness, the traditional host may no longer be able to fulfill hosting duties, but may be reluctant to admit it, knowing that it would cause consternation in the family. Then, too, younger family members, who traditionally have minimal holiday responsibilities, may want to expand their roles now that they're grown. Hosting an affair would be tangible evidence that they're accepted as mature, worthy members of the family.

What all these hypothetical situations demonstrate is that a variety of needs—some harmonious, some conflicting—intersect around the hosting question. No single approach works for every family, and no single approach will work for your family every year.

Get together with your relatives to discuss hosting duties for the next holiday. Encourage your relatives to be candid about their desires and needs. Once everything is on the table, you can move to a decision that makes the most sense for most family members. As your conversation progresses, you may even find that new options emerge. For instance, one family member can host the Thanksgiving dinner, while another can handle Christmas/Hanukkah chores, or perhaps all family members will decide to pitch in to help the host by bringing covered dishes. Hosting is one tradition that can get a healthy boost from a healthy discussion.

10.

Oh Tannenbaum!

The Christmas tree is among the most wonderful and memorable of holiday traditions, but creating that enduring symbol can be a principal source of holiday stress. Acquiring the right tree, erecting it, pruning it where necessary, watering it, and otherwise caring for it can be laborious and worrisome. If you've collected a treasure trove of ornaments through the years, one tree might not be enough to showcase your entire collection. You might feel compelled to decorate one tree downstairs, one upstairs, one in the kitchen—the list goes on.

Even if all goes well and you don't fall victim to tree inflation, you must build several days into your holiday schedule simply for this aspect of the celebration. Should things go wrong—the angel won't sit right atop the tree no matter how much you fuss with it, the tree sheds its needles prematurely, the cats use your tree as a scratching post, your municipality says it no longer will pick up used trees deposited on the curb—your tree can become an unexpected and unwelcome source of tension.

To prevent these seemingly small glitches from darkening your holidays, here's a good starting point—use only as many trees as you can accommodate without feeling anxious. If multiple trees fully trimmed work best for you, your budget, and your family, then go for them. They'll bring you pleasure rather than pressure. On the other hand, if you and your family don't think that you can handle more than a small artificial tree this year, opt for that. It will serve its purpose for you, just as a monster tree will serve its purpose for others. Circumstances and needs vary, so it's natural that trees, as well, should vary from family to family.

There may come a holiday when you can't accommodate a tree at all. This could occur because of finances, because of health conditions, or because you're traveling that season. Don't think for a minute that your holiday will be diminished. Think back to the beloved song, *O Tannenbaum*, originally a German tune with the lyric: "How true are your branches." A tree is a symbol of truth, integrity, and dedication. These are attributes we find in our hearts and minds, not in our tree stands.

11.

Here We Come Wassailing

Holiday preparation has become so hectic for us that we don't have time for door-to-door singing, much less for the rehearsal schedule that caroling might require. Yet music is a key component of our holidays. Traditional holiday tunes help link us to celebrations of the past, even as they set an appropriate mood for this year's festivities. If caroling has fallen out of favor in your community, you can do something to restore it.

Organize a group of colleagues or neighbors for caroling. If you're no musical expert, chances are that someone in your group will have the necessary experience. Invest a little time in rehearsing—it doesn't have to be much. You're not looking for a Grammy-winning performance so much as the kinship that singing can inspire. Your caroling klatch will be a welcome asset to your neighborhood or company; the singers will also benefit by becoming closer to each other. Once you've raised your voice with others in celebration, it will be much more difficult to raise your voice at them in anger.

12.

That's a Wrap

For many of us, the gift exchange is the most gratifying part of holidays—until we remember that we must wrap all of the gifts that we purchase. If you're creatively challenged, you can get emotionally wrapped up in wrapping, so much so that it becomes a persistent worry.

The more gifts you buy, the deeper your funk becomes. You find that containers and gifts are mismatched, so that nothing fits in the boxes that you picked out. There's always too much wrapping paper or not enough. Each time that you straighten the ribbon on one side of the package, it snarls on the other side. The protective "peanuts" packed by the gift shippers have been scattered throughout the room, courtesy of your pets. And finally, just when it seems that you're about to finish this thankless task, you run out of tape and must hurry to the convenience store to buy one last dispenser.

If this is your recurring holiday nightmare, step back and take a deep breath. Consider the alternative of professionally wrapped gifts. Many stores offer this feature, and you usually can request it from catalog retailers, although it may cost you a little extra. Sure, wrapping your gifts yourself is a nice personal touch that indicates the care that you've brought to the item, but if wrapping leaves you unraveled, delegate it to the pros.

Wrapping isn't any more than packaging; no matter how attractive it is, it will be discarded in a few seconds, once your family begins opening gifts. Much more important is the consideration that you lavish on all your gift recipients. If it will make your holidays less stressful, wrap up your wrapping misadventures, and do so without guilt.

13.

Deck the Halls—
and Everything Else

Decorating our homes with seasonal displays and effects can be an enduring joy of any holiday. Whether it's spider webs for Halloween, menorahs for Hanukkah, or lights, candles, crèches, and plastic reindeer for Christmas, this is a task that really can occupy us. If we choose, we can devote many hours to decorating the house, the lawn, and the trees. We even can go up on the rooftop to add a little holiday color where it will be most visible.

The neat thing about holiday decorating is that if you begin the task soon enough, the fruits of your labors can last for several weeks. You can enjoy your handiwork each day and know that you're also brightening the holiday for neighbors and passersby. Some people derive so much pleasure from their gaily festooned homes that they leave their decorations up throughout the year. That can be a real time-saver—one less task for the busy holiday crunch.

Be that as it may, the phenomenon of holiday decorating can raise your anxiety level. This may happen if you view decorating as a pressure-packed progression. You begin with modest baubles the first year, trim your outdoor trees the next year, and light the steps and walkway in year three. The need to improve each year is so great that you finally create the pièce de resistance—a life-sized re-creation of the manger, complete with shepherds and wise men.

If you can pull it off successfully, great, but if you don't have the time or resources to enhance your decorations each year, it's too easy to be disappointed in your holiday, and to regard yourself as a failure for letting your family down in this key area. It's much better and much less stressful to regard decorating as a nice touch, an add-on, rather than as a requirement. There's no need to progress to an ever-more-grand display each year. Rather, holiday decorating should be a function of the resources, time, and assistance available to you. For some holidays, you'll have ample supplies of all three, and you can get as fancy as you want. For other holidays, different priorities will demand your energy and finances, making less ornate displays the only reasonable approach.

Your holiday decorations should be as elaborate as your current circumstances allow. Don't worry if the result isn't quite as flashy as last year's. Whatever you do will be appreciated and remembered.

14.

Create New Traditions

Holiday traditions are like warm blankets; we wrap ourselves in traditions for comfort and protection from the unknown. They're so satisfying and familiar to us that we may be reluctant to change them. We always celebrate at Mom's house. We always prepare the same dishes. We always sing the same songs, and we always watch the same television shows.

As gratifying as this predictability is, think how much more rewarding holidays can be if you blend your cherished customs with new traditions—practices that you devise yourself and for which you take responsibility. Innovations can give holidays an exciting new feel and look.

For example, if you have a tree each Christmas, you may assign each family member the task of creating one new ornament each year. If you're responsible for the Thanksgiving meal, you can resolve to prepare one fantastic new dish each year to surprise and delight your family.

When you develop new traditions, everyone in the family has a stake in observing and celebrating. It's not just the host who has important duties—everybody plays a part in creating new customs. You'll also keep your holiday celebrations from becoming stale. Everyone will look forward to them with a tingle of anticipation. They'll know they're about to celebrate in time-honored ways, but they won't know exactly what to expect in the way of innovations.

New traditions will give holidays your family's personal stamp—you can be sure that no one else will celebrate in just the way that you do. Finally, by departing from the norm, you'll be introducing change and preparing your family for the changes that life inevitably brings. When you encourage your family to create and enjoy new holiday traditions, they may become more resilient as a result.

15.

Give Yourself a Stress Test

Holidays ought to be the high points of your year. Why is it, then, that they are often accompanied by exhaustion, stress, and resentment? A significant reason may be the unrealistic burdens that we impose on ourselves. We're so determined to create the perfect holiday for our loved ones that we load up on tasks that can't be accomplished very easily, at least not without giving us a bad case of jangled nerves.

As you prepare for the next holiday, it might be a good idea to give yourself a stress test—not the medical exam that has you working on a treadmill, but a homemade test that can measure your anxiety level. Here are some questions to ask yourself:

- Do you find yourself reacting angrily to small changes in plans, such as a dietary restriction that one of your guests failed to mention until now or a new travel schedule for some of your relatives?

- Do you snap at people who offer to help, determined to do it all yourself?
- Are you getting positively obsessive about secondary features of the holiday, such as decorations?
- Do you find yourself wishing that it could all be over so you could at last relax?

If you answer "yes" to these telltale questions, you've flunked your own stress test. However, it's not too late to improve your score and relieve your anxiety. Dial back a bit. Accept help when it's offered. Don't worry inordinately about peripheral matters; chances are that those things will work out fine. Once you ease up, you'll find that you're better able to accommodate changes in plans without going ballistic.

Perhaps the most important step in easing your tension is to remember that your celebration will be a complete success only if all participants—including and especially you—enjoy it. That won't be possible if you're already wishing that the holiday were over.

16.

Holidays at the Office

Holidays can add a festive air to any office. When you and your colleagues enliven your work space with seasonal decorations and plan special events for the staff, your job can play a surprisingly vital role in your holiday enjoyment. You may want to follow a few common-sense guidelines to ensure that everyone shares equally in that enjoyment, and that one worker's celebration doesn't become another's irritation.

First, it's useful to remember that what you may regard as your personal space doesn't really belong to you. It's been assigned to you by your employer, but it remains the property of the company. It's unlikely that anyone will object to your decorating your office or cubicle to your taste, unless it involves punching holes in walls or otherwise altering the furnishings. Many employers have rules regarding wall hangings and other displays. It might be best to review those before you begin decking the office halls.

Remember also that you work in close proximity to others who may not appreciate holiday music emanating from your CD player eight hours a day. Maintain a reasonable decibel level. A little consideration for others will go a long way in helping you celebrate appropriately at the office—and you have every right to expect that same consideration in return.

Some of your colleagues may not observe holidays in the same ways that you do. Indeed, large groups of employees typically encompass a broad range of beliefs and religious persuasions. You may or may not be aware of special days celebrated by your coworkers. Remember to treat your company as a melting pot of religions and ideologies when it comes to decorating. For example, common areas—such as conference rooms and lobbies—should be treated as everyone's property and reflect an ecumenical approach. That same philosophy should guide outdoor signage and displays. These represent your company to the community, so you want to participate in the holiday spirit without being offensive. If you make holidays at work as inclusive as possible, you'll be striking just the right harmonious note.

17.

Is an Office Bash
Appropriate?

For a variety of reasons, the office holiday party has become something of an endangered species. Where once companies hosted expensive bashes at some of the swankiest spots in town, many contemporary office parties are low-key affairs—if they're even held at all.

The sagging economy during the first few years of this century certainly contributed to the decline of the office party. If slumping sales forced an employer to downsize, it hardly was appropriate to lavish money on a holiday party. People were losing their jobs—not the best time for a celebration. Fear of liability has dampened holiday spirits even further. More than a few companies became quite concerned about their legal and financial responsibilities if accidents resulted from too much excess at office parties.

If planning the office holiday party is your responsibility—either individually or as part of a committee—concerns about liability and the company's financial performance are legitimate, but they shouldn't be a cause of undue stress. There are ways that you can bring your colleagues together that don't incur major costs or liabilities.

Consider, for example, a luncheon affair—either as an entire company or by departments. Alcohol consumption likely won't be an issue here, and the costs can be reasonable enough for most companies. A gift exchange—with a modest price ceiling—can be a fun part of the event.

If your organization is small enough, think of a potluck dinner at the home of one of your group or at a sensibly priced venue. There's virtually no cost involved, and everyone still can enjoy the spirit of the season.

The keys to a successful office party are to enjoy the company of your colleagues, to get to know their families and introduce yours to them, and to observe the holidays with people you love and respect. You can accomplish all that without renting out the ritziest place in town.

18.

Surviving
Gift Exchanges

On its surface, the holiday gift exchange is an unpretentious and uncomplicated way of celebrating at the office. Yet even this seemingly innocuous way of observing the holiday and saluting your colleagues can send your blood pressure soaring.

What happens, you might wonder, if you stay under the gift price ceiling imposed by the event's organizers, but your someone presents you with something more expensive? Will you look stingy in the eyes of your coworkers? Will you appear dull and uninventive because you let your purchase be dictated by an arbitrary ceiling that everyone else ignored?

If you transcend the price limit, will you embarrass a gift recipient who stayed beneath the ceiling, or perhaps have your colleagues think that you're trying to draw attention to yourself with an overly generous purchase? What about the gift itself? Clothes might be too intimate, alcohol too offensive, specialty foods uninspired.

If you find yourself going through these gift-exchange gymnastics, relax. The gift exchange is designed to be a small pleasure in the holiday season, not an opportunity to earn public relations points or fret about proper protocol. What's most important is the quality of the thought involved, not the actual gift.

Instead of worrying, spend your time pondering what small item your colleague would most appreciate, and then buy it. Of course you should try to stay under the price ceiling, but if you're a little over, don't worry. When you select your gift thoughtfully, the price won't matter.

19.

Office Party Protocol

What's intriguing about office parties is that they occur within the confines of the office. Even those held off site still play out under the umbrella of the company and its rules—both formal and informal. The people who report to you will be there; your superiors will be on hand, as well. That means any comment that you make can reverberate throughout the company and affect your work relationships. In short, even though you're celebrating, you're under scrutiny—and perhaps scrutinizing others, too.

Excessive caution can be as damaging as excessive revelry. Office parties are not held in a political vacuum, but that shouldn't create undue anxiety for you. Your company likes you. They're fans of your work and your personality—that's why they hired you, and that's why they've promoted you and supported you all of these years.

If it's your personality to tell a joke, tell it with style. If you usually prefer to listen while others talk, listen attentively. The best thing to be at your office party is yourself.

20.

Remembering Your Colleagues

Presenting gifts to coworkers who have helped you through the year seems to be a wonderful way to acknowledge the people who've shared your highs, supported you through the lows, and generally brightened your work environment. Noble as your intentions may be, holiday gifts for your colleagues can get caught up in a swirl of office politics, turning your good intentions into a source of unwelcome holiday stress.

It seems crazy that such a simple notion—providing tangible evidence of your gratitude and best wishes—must be viewed through the filter of office etiquette. Yet the larger your company, the more likely it is that your gifts to colleagues will be analyzed and debated. If that sort of scrutiny is unavoidable, then you may want to follow a few common-sense guidelines in bestowing gifts on your colleagues.

First, simple gifts are best. Expensive presents will set the gossip mill churning. If you have a special relationship with a colleague and want to recognize that with something pricey, it might be better to present your gift away from the office. Think of small items that express appreciation. If you bake, a dozen cookies for each of your most valued colleagues accompanied by a nice note would be appropriate and appreciated. If you're also able to leave a few dozen in conference rooms and the cafeteria so that everyone might enjoy your cookies, you'll be spreading your cheer far and wide without triggering any negative reaction.

If you are in a supervisory position, it's probably a bad idea to use holiday gifts as a way of rewarding or censuring your employees for their performance during the year. Performance reviews always should be thorough, they always should allow for give and take, and they always should be conducted in private. If you reward your best employees with handsome fruit baskets but give the laggards nothing but stress balls, you'll in effect be issuing public job appraisals that soon will be the talk of the shop floor.

Spread your good wishes equally among your employees. Save your comments about their performances for a more suitable occasion.

21.

Double Time
Versus Quality Time

Here's a classic holiday dilemma that many people will face at some point in their careers. You're planning a nice, cozy gathering for a big holiday when the boss offers you the opportunity to work that day. The company really needs you, but even more attractive is the premium pay that you'll earn for hours worked on the holiday. Which do you opt for—double time or quality time?

The answer isn't as uncomplicated as it may appear. Some will turn down the big payday, believing that there's nothing more important than spending holidays with family, no matter the financial sacrifice. However, what if, in giving up one holiday, you can ease some of the financial pressure on your family and help ensure that future holidays are happy? In that case, wouldn't it make sense to accept the work assignment? Besides, you can celebrate with your family once you knock off work.

As these questions indicate, this is a delicate decision that can leave you frustrated and feeling guilty, no matter which option you select. One way to assure that you make the best choice is to discuss the matter with your family. Get a read on their feelings, and make your decision accordingly. If you chart a course of action together, chances are that all of you will avoid feeling bad about the choice.

Remember that the right answer for this holiday might be the wrong answer for the next holiday. Circumstances can change rapidly. A few extra dollars today might seem a nice luxury, discretionary income that will come in handy. Tomorrow, that cash infusion might be an absolute necessity. There is no right or wrong choice, but if you keep your family in the loop, you may find that double time and quality time aren't mutually exclusive.

22.
Choosing Gifts Thoughtfully

Purchasing gifts can be a particularly trying aspect of holidays and a source of considerable anxiety. Making sure that you have enough money for your purchases—or conversely, buying only those gifts that you can afford—is tough enough, but the gift gauntlet goes beyond that.

Selecting just the right gift for everyone on your list may be the biggest challenge of all. Should it be a practical present or one just for fun? Should it be expensive or reasonably priced? If it is expensive, does that mean you must shell out for comparably priced gifts for everyone else so that no one will feel slighted?

Then there are questions of venue. If you do your shopping at the mall, you know that you'll walk away with your gift in hand, but you'll also have to endure travel time, parking difficulties, and potentially long lines at the checkout. You can avoid all that with catalog or e-mail purchases, but then you'll be forced to sweat out delivery of the gifts.

Mix in such matters as worries about the proper sizing, appropriate wrapping, and on-time mailing if you're sending to folks out of town, and the gift exchange can become a significant energy burner. If you had any idea how much time and creativity gifts would require, you might have avoided this tradition in the first place and opted for a cards-only holiday!

Of course, you're not likely to abandon gift-giving—nor should you—but you *can* introduce a less stressful approach. Once you have your list together, spend the bulk of your time thinking about which gifts your recipients would most value and appreciate. This is where you want to direct most of your creativity. Think of this as your "concept list." If you're clear on the concepts, you can refine them by browsing store aisles and catalog pages to get the right selections within your concepts.

From here, the rest of the process is much easier than with the time-honored approach. It doesn't matter whether your purchases come from chic boutiques or discount department stores, whether they cost a lot or a little, whether they're professionally packaged or hand-wrapped. The important thing is that you've selected your gifts thoughtfully, prioritizing the satisfaction of your recipients rather than some arbitrary cost guidelines.

Chances are that your beneficiaries will be so delighted with their gifts that they won't give a second thought to where you bought them or what they cost. When that happens, you'll know that you have this gift thing down pat.

23.

Shop Till You Drop?

Of all the traditions associated with holidays, perhaps none is more potentially stressful than gift shopping for friends and relatives. It doesn't have to be this way. Choosing special gifts for those near and dear to us, wrapping the presents ourselves as we anticipate the joy that they'll bring, watching that joy as it lights the faces of the recipients—all that should be a rewarding experience. Too often, though, the satisfaction of the gift exchange is diminished or wiped out by our insecurity that we're not giving enough.

Instead of committing some quality time to determine what gifts will work best for each family member, we look first at price tags to make sure that we're spending enough to adequately express our affection—as if love could be measured in dollars. So we make price-directed purchases. Then, as the holiday nears, we fear that we haven't bought enough, so we hit the mall once more. Even then, we're not done because we realize that by spending more on one family member, we may slight other loved ones who'll receive less. There's only one way to relieve the panic—buy still more. This sort of shop-till-you-drop cycle takes all of the joy out of gift giving.

A better approach might be to let your gift decisions be guided by what you might call the usefulness/delight scale. Will your loved ones find your gifts useful and practical? Will they beam with delight when they open your presents? If the answer to either question is yes, you may have the right gifts. If you answer both questions in the affirmative, you know that you have winners, no matter what price the gifts were.

If you end up spending more on one family member than another, chances are that your loved ones won't even realize it because they appreciate your gifts so much. For your painstaking efforts, you'll emerge with something valuable, as well—the joy of giving without price pressure.

24.

The Mall and Alternate Venues

Like it or not, much of the focus of holiday shopping has shifted to the mall. A large shopping plaza offers the advantages of convenience and efficiency. On paper, at least, we can attend to our grocery and gift shopping, as well as meet some of our everyday needs—all in one fell swoop.

Viewed less charitably, the mall can be a plaza of pressure where various sources of holiday stress are gathered under one roof: heavy traffic, parking woes, picked-over merchandise, and long lines of cranky customers at the register. All of these things can transform a potentially exciting holiday outing into a giant headache.

If mall shopping introduces a sense of dread to your holiday, consider alternate venues. Shopping by catalog is workable for many goods, particularly if you don't feel the need to visually inspect them or touch them before purchasing. Most catalog merchants are respectable and reliable; they offer a customer service phone number that you can call should difficulties arise.

E-mail can be another way to go. You may consider "e-tailers" still too new for your more cautious approach, but shopping online has grown impressively. Thousands of shoppers are now clicking their way to holiday gifts.

Not all purchases lend themselves to this "hands-off" methodology, and shopping by catalog and e-mail can involve a bit more planning and time. You'll want to give yourself a cushion so that there's adequate time to correct any problems, but you'll avoid the frenzy of last-minute shopping and the frustrations of the mall.

If you employ alternate venues to conclude your shopping early, take a leisurely trip to the mall to soak up the sights and sounds of the season. It's amazing how much less stressful your visit will be when you know that your shopping, much like a gift to yourself, is wrapped up.

25.

A Holiday Lesson
from History

On many holidays, we solemnly wish for "peace on earth." Though our hope for harmony is genuine, it seems such an unattainable dream that we may well retreat to our holiday traditions without thinking much about this lofty objective. When we feel that goal slipping away, we might well remember the Christmas Truce of 1914, one of the most astonishing events in the history of war—if not the history of man.

With World War I well underway, British and German troops found themselves dug in across a no-man's land on Christmas Day. It's not clear how the truce began, although it was neither ordered by British or German high command nor officially sanctioned at any point. Before long, soldiers on both sides were meeting under white flags in the no-man's land in what became a remarkable Christmas armistice.

In their book *Christmas Truce* (as excerpted by PBS), Malcolm Brown and Shirley Seaton note that soldiers trying to kill each other only a few hours before stood between their respective trenches, shaking hands and exchanging addresses and cigarettes. It was not the only spontaneous holiday armistice in the history of war, but it was the most spectacular—and the most widely noted. Sir Arthur Conan Doyle called it "one human episode amid all the atrocities which have stained the memory of war."

The Christmas Truce should not be misinterpreted as an antiwar protest by the soldiers who participated, or even a reaction against particular strategies or tactics. Indeed, hostilities resumed shortly after Christmas, and truce participants knew that was as it had to be.

What the truce represents is the fleeting transcendence of brotherhood against all odds, inspired by a sacred day and a common vision of the way that things could be. For a moment, people's best instincts triumphed. For a moment each holiday, we can pay homage to these brave soldiers by imagining that our noble instincts will be triumphant again—and by committing ourselves to that dream.

26.

Solo Doesn't Mean "So Low"

We usually think of holidays as occasions for togetherness, when families gather from distant locales to share the warmth that has nurtured them through the years. For those living alone, though, that option may not be available.

It's no secret that holidays can be depressing for singles. When they see the familial warmth that others are enjoying and compare that to their own situation, they easily can become discouraged. Holidays may seem especially bleak for those separated from their families by distance, divorce, or death, but even those who are single by choice may feel a twinge of holiday sadness when they observe others experiencing a type of joy that will elude them again.

If you're solo for a holiday, that doesn't mean you have to be "so low." Holidays can be as warm and memorable for you as they are for those in family situations. Rather than allow yourself to slip into a comforting but unproductive nostalgia for the holidays of yesteryear, take the initiative to make the current holiday memorable.

Send out holiday cards. This custom is as valuable for singles as it is for families. Your efforts will probably yield many cards in return, and your greeting cards might even prompt old friends to call and enliven your holiday with their conversation. If they don't call you, take the next step and contact them. Spend some time with them. You might even arrange a holiday gathering of old friends who find themselves without family. Who knows? Your initiative might inspire a holiday gathering that could become a tradition for you and your buddies.

You also can spend part of your holiday with community organizations, assisting those in need. If you help prepare meals for the hungry and shelter for the homeless, your contribution to the holiday can be significant, indeed.

Finally, if you're invited to spend the holiday with the family of a friend or relative, accept the offer eagerly. Your initial inclination might be to spurn the invitation because you suspect that it is offered in pity, or because you fear that you'll feel—and be perceived as—an outsider. Accept this generosity as an opportunity to enrich your holiday—and to enhance the holiday for others through your presence and good will.

27.

Get Your Kids Involved

Holidays are for children—and for the children inside all adults.
Our elaborate preparations often are designed to ensure the
happiest holidays possible for our children. That's a selfless goal, but
it doesn't mean that the young ones should be passive participants in
holidays. Getting your kids involved—at whatever level makes sense
to them—will instill in them the spirit of holidays. They may not be
able to fully articulate their understanding and appreciation now;
they'll show it years later, when they stage holiday affairs for their
own children.

You can bring your kids into the loop in a variety of ways. The
youngest children can accompany you to the supermarket and help
you pick out your holiday groceries. They may not be able to afford
gifts yet, but they can come with you when you select the presents
that ostensibly come from them. Kids can also pitch in to set the table
and clean up after the meal.

As your children grow, they can help in still other ways, such as
cleaning the house, trimming the tree, and placing decorations.

They can wrap the gifts they'll be presenting and sing along with you when you're out caroling.

Your children can make a valuable contribution to your holiday cards. If you traditionally include a letter updating friends and family on developments in your household, get your kids to help you list the happenings to be noted. Better yet, assign them to write the letter themselves. Many children will jump at the chance to compose and produce such letters on their computers. It will be a fun and useful task for them, as they'll be improving their composition, computing, and desktop publishing skills.

Whatever their particular chores, it's important to establish some significant role for your children. The more active they are now, the higher their self-esteem will soar. Holidays will be that much more meaningful for them—now and in the years to come.

28.

What About Santa Claus?

As parents, each of us faces the day when we must confirm the hard truth for our kids about one of the most revered figures in their lives. He's a man of warmth, mystery, and incredible energy—and now we must tell our children that he doesn't really exist. Santa Claus is as much cultural icon as he is a religious figure. Even those who don't formally celebrate Christmas face the uncomfortable prospect of Santa D-Day.

Don't worry unduly about the timing of your heart-to-heart with your kids; they'll most likely determine the timing for you. They'll hear it first from a classmate, a precocious cynic who takes delight in spreading the news. Your kids will stew about it all day as they shift nervously at their desks. Then when they come home, the question will positively burst from their lips: Is it true that there is no Santa Claus?

You've been dreading this day, of course, because it represents an end to the phase of childhood when all things are possible. It doesn't mean that your children are grown, or that you won't have many more experiences to share with them, but it might be time for this particular lesson.

If they're ready to move past Santa, there's little to be gained by perpetuating the myth any longer. You might be tempted to do that for your benefit, to preserve their golden childhood a bit longer. Still, you want to let them down gently. A useful approach is to explain that while Santa Claus isn't a real person, he exists in our minds and hearts as a symbol of all that is good about us as humans—our generosity, our sense of humor, our concern for others. Santa Claus is the spirit of everything that we hope to be, and that's why he continues to be such a powerful and lasting legend for us.

With a bit of sensitivity, your heart-to-heart about Santa can serve to reinforce the spirit of Christmas for your kids. They'll accept it, they'll grow with the knowledge, and you'll have witnessed the Christmas miracle that somehow recurs with every generation.

29.

Should Children
Have Gift Lists?

Along with mistletoe, holly, and chestnuts roasting on an open fire, gift lists compiled for us by our children have become standard trappings of the holiday season. When you get a look at the list, it may be so dominated by techno-gadgetry that you may think you're being asked to equip a space station rather than satisfy your kids. The list usually is a pretty fair indication that you'll be spending considerable time and money this holiday season.

Resist the temptation to toss the list on the open fire with the chestnuts. Given the hard sell of toys and technology by the nation's retailers, there's an inevitability to gift lists. It would be an unusual child who could ignore the media barrage and focus on other aspects of the holidays. If you initiate the discussion by asking your young ones what they would like for the holidays, you really have no one to blame but yourself when they respond—in chapter and verse.

So gift lists from your children may be unavoidable, but perhaps there are ways you can transform those lists to multifunctional tools. First, ask your kids to prioritize their wishes so that you don't purchase something from the "B" list and disappoint them. Next, make sure that your kids are as specific as they can be about their preferences. This will be especially vital with technology-based items. If this year's release of a popular video game is all the rage, it's a good bet that last year's is passé. It will be important for your kids to convey the correct makes, model numbers, and releases if you're to present them with exactly the gifts that they want.

Next, don't be bound by your kids' wishes. Their lists will cover what they want, but it's unlikely that your children will address what they need. Don't feel guilty about working sweaters, scarves, and gloves into the hit parade. If you're able to blend what your kids want with what they need, you can score on both fronts.

Finally, advise your kids that if they plan to compile gift lists, they also must create "give" lists—the names of family and friends to whom they plan to present gifts, along with some idea of what those gifts will be. This will serve to introduce them to the reciprocity of holiday giving and broaden their perspective a bit. You still may have to help them finance their purchases, but if their "give" lists get them thinking of others in addition to themselves, you'll have achieved an important holiday goal.

30.

Cut the Kids Some Slack

Holidays often serve as milestones in the development of our children as unique people. There's that Easter when they stopped believing in the bunny, that fateful Halloween when they decided that trick-or-treating was kid stuff, and that memorable Christmas when they gave up Santa once and for all. We typically recall these watershed holidays with mixed emotions. We're delighted and proud to see our children mature, yet we wish that they somehow could retain the innocence and wonder of their formative years.

When your kids become teenagers, you may be entering uncharted territory where holidays are concerned. Their lives are distinct from yours now in a number of important ways; what they want most is to carve out their own identities, spend time with their own friends, and pursue their own activities. Their quest for individuality may conflict with your desire for family holidays as usual. When you need them for holiday preparation, they're off at band practice, at a soccer match, or socializing with their friends. This can lead to arguments within the family if you don't identify the conflict and address it with firmness and understanding.

Be firm about those holiday obligations that you regard as near-sacred, such as trimming the tree together or conducting the Passover seder as a family unit. Let your teens know that they *will* participate in these events, and that absences *will not* be tolerated.

Be understanding about less important aspects of the holiday. Your kids may be your traditional helpers in decorating the house. If they need to be with their friends this year instead of helping you, cut them some slack. Teenagers need freedom *and* rules; the wise parent provides both.

One way of doing so is to encourage your kids to invite friends over to participate in holiday preparations—and in holidays themselves. This works particularly well when your children's mates don't celebrate the same holidays as you, or they celebrate the same holidays in different ways. You'll broaden the experience of young people—who might well extend that tradition when they stage their own holiday celebrations as adults.

31.

When the Kids Are Grown

Much of the hard work that we invest in holiday planning is for the benefit of our children. Not only do we want them to enjoy these special occasions, but we also want them to know how much they're loved and valued. What better way to show it than by going out of our way to plan magical celebrations that will delight them? Of course, we take back more than our share of satisfaction when we see the wonder light their faces, bright as Christmas candles.

Inevitably, though, your kids grow and leave home, some for far distant locales. That doesn't mean that your holiday planning and celebrations should end. In fact, the more far-flung your family, the more important holidays can become.

Holidays may be the one time when you can reunite everyone and bask again in the warmth of family. It takes more planning, more coordination, more compromising than ever to bring the family together when the kids are scattered. To get everyone in the same place at the same time, you may even have to observe the holiday before or after it actually occurs. If your schedules make that necessary, don't worry about being out of step with the rest of the world. Any day that you can reunite your family is an occasion worth celebrating.

If your kids can't make it, you'll be able to enjoy a holiday celebration of a different order. When it's just the two of you, your event can take on a quiet, more reflective tone. You can dial back on gifts and decorations if you want. You can also travel for the holiday—perhaps something that you've always wanted to do but couldn't, for the kids' sake.

The growth of your children may change the character of your holiday, but it can usher in a new type of celebration that can be equally satisfying in a novel way. The joy never needs to stop.

32.

Over the River and
Through the Woods

Modern travel options are at once the beauty and bane of contemporary holidays. Traveling on the interstate is great—unless the highway is closed due to weather or construction. Air travel also is terrific—but if a loved one's flight is canceled or detoured, what happens then to your well-timed holiday affair?

You—and those coming to visit—should finalize holiday travel plans as soon as possible. That will give everyone plenty of time to consider alternatives if problems arise.

Most importantly, be flexible in your planning. If you're thinking, "Mom and Dad are coming on a flight that takes two hours, so we can eat dinner at six," you may be sorely frustrated when your parents are grounded at their airport. A better approach is, "Best case is that Mom and Dad will be here in two hours, but if not, we'll start whenever they arrive." Now, you're prepared for just about everything.

33.

You're an Angel

There may be no better way to observe a holiday than by extending the celebration to our neediest citizens. You can reach out by becoming an angel tree benefactor.

Angel trees are projects of nonprofit organizations, often in association with an important local employer. Each "ornament" on the tree is the name of a child who might not receive any gifts except for those provided by you. The ornaments usually include the first name, clothing sizes, and perhaps gift preferences of the children. Your role is to purchase and wrap a gift, although sometimes the lead organization provides wrapping services. You can buy for one child, for three, or for as many as you would like.

The sponsoring group may invite you to its party so that you can make your presentation in person. Many times, though, their celebrations are private for medical reasons, or because anonymity must be preserved. Even if you're not on hand to witness it, you can imagine the look of wonder and delight that your gift generates.

Angel trees are one vehicle for ensuring that all kids have the opportunity to experience holiday joy, but there are many others. Perhaps your local food pantry is staging a holiday drive, or the hospital in your region is soliciting for its free-care fund. Even donating blood during holidays, when many blood banks experience chronic shortages, is a useful contribution. Although you may not reap the satisfaction that a one-to-one gift brings, supporting these causes can go a long way toward brightening holidays in your community.

If you can't identify a project such as these in your town, why not initiate one? When you contact a local nonprofit organization, they'll probably be thrilled to work with you. They may have some guidelines that you might not have considered previously, but these shouldn't impede your mission, and then you won't have to worry about doing it all yourself. Inform your colleagues of your goal, and they'll step right up to help. Once you plant and nurture your angel tree, all your friends and coworkers will want to earn their wings.

34.

Gifts Without Guilt

Presenting and receiving gifts can be a gratifying holiday tradition for all involved. You bestow on a friend or loved one something valuable—a gift your recipient had only dreamed of owning—and you get a similar treasure in return. Yet even something as mutually beneficial as exchanging gifts can be a source of holiday anxiety.

Stress can mount when the value of gifts exchanged is out of whack. If you present people with expensive gifts but receive mere baubles from them in return, there's a tendency to feel slighted. You dug deep into your pocket to please your loved ones. Couldn't they have done the same for you?

Alternately, you may be on the receiving end of a terrific present that makes the trinket that you gave pale by comparison. Embarrassed, you ponder ways to make up the difference and realize that it's too late to do much of anything about the situation, at least for now.

This sort of frustration is more likely to afflict you if you measure the success of any holiday by the dollar value of gifts. With the media assault on our shopping sensibilities, it's understandable to perceive holidays as a sort of commercial contest. This is a temptation that we must resist.

We present gifts because we love our family and friends, because we want to bring pleasure to their lives, and because we want to be there to share that pleasure with them. Those who present us with gifts have much the same agenda. If you and your family achieve these goals, your gift exchange will be a success—no matter how much any particular present cost.

When you give a more expensive gift than you receive, don't stress about it. You brought happiness to a loved one, which may be the most important goal of all. When someone lavishes a wickedly expensive gift on you, accept it without guilt. Someone you love thinks that you deserve it.

35.

I Love It! What Is It?

It happens every holiday, doesn't it? The box grabs your attention; the wrapping paper is so colorful and enticing that you know you must save this gift for last. Trembling with anticipation, you rip through the packaging only to find…a sweatsuit that's clearly two sizes too large for you; or a hideous tie that couldn't possibly match anything in your wardrobe; or a tempting box of milk chocolates that would wreak havoc with the diet that you have resolved to begin with the new year. That smile of anticipation is frozen on your face as you struggle to find the words of gratitude that you don't feel.

This is fairly standard holiday fare. It's difficult enough to match the right gifts with the right people. If someone is shopping for many family members and friends, it's hard to lavish adequate time and resources on just that special present for you. If you're on the receiving end of a well-intentioned white elephant and find your disappointment rising, it may be a good time to reorder your holiday priorities.

First, think back to all the gifts that you've presented over the years, including those seasons when you were rushed and picked up whatever you could find at the last minute. Doubtless, some of the presents that you bestowed resulted in the same letdown that you're feeling now. Remember your own predicament, and you'll empathize with loved ones who struggled to come up with the perfect gift for you.

If your primary expectation for any holiday is the material items that you'll receive, you may need to adjust your attitude. We all know that it's better to give than to receive, but receiving gifts graciously can be just as important as giving them generously. If someone thinks enough of you to allocate precious time and money for a gift, you already have something more valuable than whatever might be in the box.

So when you get that ghastly tie, wear it proudly—and pick an occasion when the person who gave it to you will see it. Who cares if you clash? What's important is the appreciation that you'll be expressing—a treasure that only you can give.

36.

The Fruitcake Conundrum

Fruitcake has been given a bad name. This beleaguered baked good has come to symbolize all of the unwanted, inappropriate, ill-fitting holiday gifts that we've received—and given—over the years. Even people who never have received a fruitcake can commiserate with those who get them regularly. Everyone knows that this is one gift that does not take the cake.

For all that, there's method to the fruitcake madness. First, many people genuinely like this food; for them, fruitcake is a gift that will be ingested rather than protested.

Even beyond that, fruitcake represents the ultimate in a safe gift, the type we usually present to people that we want to acknowledge but with whom we may be less than intimate. What do you do with the folks at the tail end of your gift list? You don't want to spend a lot of money on them. You can't give them apparel, since you don't know their sizes, and gifts of clothing might not be proper anyway. Liquor is out of the question—you're not familiar with their drinking habits or preferences. Cash, we're told, is a cold, impersonal gift, so that's out. What remains? Fruitcake! It's the torte of last resort.

There's nothing wrong with fruitcake in these situations, as long as you have an inkling that the recipients will like it. You have many other options, though, for folks you want to acknowledge while staying within your holiday budget. Gift certificates can be a productive option. You'll want to avoid selecting a certificate to a sporting goods store, for example, unless you're sure that the beneficiary is the outdoorsy type, but almost everyone will appreciate a gift certificate to the supermarket or the movies. No matter the amount of the certificate, it's money that you've returned to your friends' pockets.

You can customize your gift certificates to each friend's circumstances. A friend who works at home might receive a certificate to an office supply store. A friend who travels many highway miles can use a certificate from the local auto club. It won't take much ingenuity on your part to resolve the fruitcake conundrum. As for fruitcakes that you receive, nothing much to be done about those. *Bon appétit!*

37.

Seconds Anyone?

Preparing the holiday meal can be a source of great satisfaction—or frustration, depending on how things go around the dinner table. One of the great advantages about being the designated cook for your family's celebration is that the chore can be stretched for days or even a few weeks. You need time to plan the menu, consult with your guests about any special dietary needs, and shop at supermarkets and food boutiques to get the right ingredients at the right prices.

On most days, meals are devoured in seconds, so your satisfaction as cook may be just as fleeting. Holiday meals are more complicated, the fare more varied. You can devote so much time to preparation and to the anticipation of your guests' delight that your experience becomes a four-phase exercise in satisfaction—planning the meal, acquiring the ingredients, cooking, and watching as your handiwork is enjoyed.

What happens, however, if the food that you lovingly prepare isn't as well received as you imagined it would be? Nobody actually criticizes any of the dishes—your family is much too polite for that—but you can sense an uneasy mood. You can't sell anybody on seconds, and the mashed potatoes and stuffing are just sitting there, virtually untouched. You're crestfallen, but you shouldn't let this mood last or consider your meal a failure.

Remember first of all that if you're cooking for a large group, it's quite unlikely that every dish will please every diner. Tastes vary, so it's natural that the responses to your cooking will cover a wide range. If your menu is diverse enough, your guests will find at least some dishes that they enjoy. It's unrealistic of you to expect more.

Also, it's wise to acknowledge that even the best, most consistent cooks falter on occasion. If something that you prepared turns out to be a holiday bust, don't sulk, don't blame yourself, and don't consider your family to be ungrateful. None of that is helpful. Instead, encourage your guests to provide you with honest critiques. Based on their feedback, you may find that you can improve the holiday meal with only minor adjustments. If you're open to suggestions, you'll have them diving in for seconds the next time around.

38.

You're Not a Restaurateur

When you see your loved ones pounce on the holiday meal that you prepared, you know that you've made this day special for them. However, being the designated cook can bring its share of pressure, as well, and limiting stress should be a universal holiday goal.

The tension begins when you try to accommodate the gustatory pleasures of all of your guests. Your spouse loves your cranberry relish, so you know that will be on the menu. One of your kids prefers turkey, the other ham, so both foods must be featured. Aunt Sally will eat nut bread as long as it doesn't have nuts, while Uncle Frank won't touch it unless it has those big walnuts. Better plan on both kinds.

This kind of menu planning can send you over the edge. Remember, you're a host, not a restaurateur. When people dine with you, they're not expecting to get "substitutions." Your efforts will be appreciated, even if you don't whip up every guest's favorite food.

It does make some sense to accommodate important personal needs. For example, medical conditions may limit the diet of some of your guests; in such cases, it's both practical and courteous to prepare foods that those on restricted diets can enjoy. Religious and philosophical restrictions also should be considered. If a guest won't eat pork for religious reasons, and another guest is a vegetarian, you would be less than a good host if you didn't prepare alternate selections for them.

Beyond these circumstances, don't worry unduly about catering to individual tastes. Your guests value your efforts as host and cook, and they'll enjoy everything that you prepare. Your meal will be a stunning success. If some of your guests offer to bring additions to the meal, don't misinterpret their generosity as a comment on your abilities. Accept their contributions graciously. Holiday meals involve more than broth, so you never can have too many cooks.

39.

Be the Perfect Guest

The spotlight during holiday gatherings usually falls on the host. This makes sense, since it's the host who's largely responsible for decorations, the holiday meal, and any activities. Far less attention is devoted to the conduct of guests who, it is sometimes assumed, can do whatever they want. They're the guests, after all. Yet most of us probably can remember a holiday celebration that was spoiled by rude or inconsiderate behavior on the part of guests. Following are just a few basic guidelines to remind us of elementary courtesy as guests.

Offer to help. Assistance can come in many forms, such as bringing a dessert, cleaning up, and helping with the dishes. Particularly useful will be your offer to transport guests who don't drive themselves. In foul weather, that can be a holiday-saver.

If your assistance is declined, don't mope. Many hosts get so deeply into their responsibilities that they spurn all offers of help, lest assistance make them seem less than capable. If your hosts have their "game faces" on, gently remind them that you're available for whatever they need, and then sit back and enjoy.

Inform your host in advance of any dietary restrictions. Your host will almost assuredly be delighted to whip up alternate fare for you— so long as you have communicated your needs in a timely fashion.

If your plans change, let your host know promptly. Your travel schedule may take a hit, or you may find that there will be one less in your traveling party, or perhaps one more. Update your host as soon as possible. Most holiday celebrations can accommodate these kinds of changes.

Follow house rules. If shoes aren't permitted on the host's carpets, walk uncomplainingly in your stocking feet. If television is taboo during dinner, live without the tube for an hour or two. Your host has labored long and hard to make this day a success for all. In response, you should be willing to endure a minor inconvenience for a brief period. That's what being the perfect guest is about.

40.

Are Holiday White Lies Okay?

We've all been in that uncomfortable situation where we know that the truth will hurt, but our natural inclination to honesty won't let us lie easily. Around holidays, such ethical dilemmas can corner us with unpleasant frequency. A loved one asks us how a new outfit looks; if the truth be known, it doesn't look so hot. A friend presents us with a gift that we don't care for and asks if we love it.

Are white lies okay in these situations? There's no right or wrong answer here, yet erring on the side of truth may be the best approach. If you impart your answers with thoughtful and careful words, you can avoid any pain or resentment.

Most people want to do the best that they can; if you can help them in that regard, so much the better. White lies may protect feelings for now, but because they conceal the truth, they rule out the possibility of improvement. Friends and family will accept your honesty, provided you offer it in the spirit of generosity. You can be diplomatic even as you remember that truth never takes a holiday.

41.

Chasing the Holiday Blahs

Holidays seem special by their very definition, but they can become stale and predictable. This may occur when you gather with the same people, eat the same fare, and watch the same television shows for so many years that there's nothing really special about the agenda. In fact, about the only thing that marks these days as different is that you don't have to report to work.

If you find your observances taking on this numbing sort of sameness, think about ways to restore the special quality of these special days. For example, a group of college students in the Northeast each year plans a special event for Martin Luther King Jr. Day. One year, they may stage a dramatic reading of King's works. The next year, equipped with buckets and brushes, they scrub away all the racist graffiti in town. They choose their happenings creatively but carefully so that whatever they do perpetuates the teachings of Martin Luther King Jr.

At the Veterans Affairs Hospital in Butler, Pennsylvania, a group of motorcycle enthusiasts has been visiting at Christmas time for years, bearing gifts for each resident. The bikers jam the parking lot with their vehicles—a spectacle in itself—and they wear their traditional gear as they spread cheer from room to room. It's a special holiday for patients and bikers alike.

In Pittsburgh, the Audubon Society of Western Pennsylvania celebrates the Christmas/New Year season by inviting residents to take part in a winter bird count. Participants don their heavy coats and boots, tramp through the woods of southwestern Pennsylvania, and help the professionals document the diversity of avian life. If that doesn't make your holiday take flight, nothing will.

Perhaps that's more exertion than you're looking for, but there are plenty of less strenuous ways to make holidays special. You can fly a flag on Flag Day, plant a tree on Arbor Day, or visit a veterans hospital on Veterans Day. If you select an activity that's consistent with the themes of the holiday, chances are that you'll chase the holiday blahs away—permanently.

42.

Invite a Vegetarian to Dinner

Holidays are a unifying force in our culture. We all celebrate Thanksgiving on the same day. At Halloween, we all outfit our kids for trick-or-treating and buy candy to distribute at our own doors. New Year's Eve always occurs on New Year's Eve, right? Not much variation there.

However, this seeming homogeneity masks a great and wonderful diversity in how we celebrate, and indeed how we view life itself. Consider the festival of Hanukkah, for example. Some celebrate it for a single evening only, while others continue the observance for a full eight days. Some treat holidays primarily as religious affairs; the centerpiece of their observance is a worship service. Others regard holidays more as time for the gathering of family and friends than as a religious event.

Who has the best idea about how to observe holidays? Each approach is as appropriate as the next. If you stick exclusively to your own traditions, you may be missing the opportunity that holidays present to broaden your experiences and learn about other ways of thinking. Now is a great time to begin taking advantage of that opportunity.

If you're planning to attend worship services, invite a family outside of your faith to join you. They'll learn about your beliefs and customs—and you can return the favor by accompanying them to their house of worship on the next holiday. When you dine with your friends after the services, you'll have many new things to discuss and compare.

If you traditionally serve meat at your holiday meal, why not invite a vegetarian to celebrate with you? You'll need to prepare alternate fare, of course, but you'll discover much about a different way of looking at life—and you may encounter some tasty new dishes, as well. If you're open to new ideas, holidays can help strengthen the bonds between you and others, even as you perpetuate your most cherished traditions.

43.

When Illness Invades
Your Holidays

In the ideal world, we're hale and hearty through every holiday; our friends and family enjoy good health, as well, so that medical concerns never cast a pall over the holiday mood. Alas, in the real world, illness has little respect for the calendar. It's quite likely that at some point in your life, you'll have to cope with the poor health of a loved one—or perhaps your own illnesses—during a holiday.

The sickness that has befallen your family may leave you feeling so low that you'd prefer to get beyond the holiday without any sort of fanfare. It just doesn't seem the right time for merriment. Yet there are times during family illness when low-key observation of a holiday still may be appropriate.

If you're the one who falls ill, you might want your family to press on and enjoy the holiday as best they can. You need to see your kids engaging in a gift exchange, however scaled-down it might be. You want their experiences and memories to be happy. If you feel that way, it's quite likely that your family members will have the same feelings should they be stricken.

Your first priority is dealing with the needs—both medical and psychological—of anyone in your family circle who is ailing. If they can't physically be with you because they're hospitalized, take the holiday to them. Plan as much of a celebration as their circumstances will allow. If you think that they'll be able to enjoy the goodies you bake each holiday, take some to them. If they'll enjoy opening gifts, take all of their presents to the bedside. (By the way, if you're celebrating at a hospital, don't forget to spread your cheer to the staff. That will help you maintain the spirit of the holiday even through your pain.) If your loved ones can't enjoy pastries and gifts, that's okay, too. Your very presence will be the best holiday gift.

Then continue to observe the holiday with the rest of your family. Celebrate to the extent the occasion will allow, but somehow, some way, celebrate. Your holiday observance will be an indication of continuity, of the perpetuation of family traditions in the face of unpredictable events, and of your cohesiveness and strength as a family unit.

44.

A Time for Healing

Family means warmth and comfort—and deeply felt emotions. We're connected to our family members through the bonds of shared experiences—but sometimes, we need to tread carefully. Maintaining family harmony can be a delicate balancing act.

If an acquaintance says something that you interpret as disparaging, you're probably able to shrug it off and go about your business without a second thought. When that same remark comes from a close friend or family member, the pain can run deep, however inoffensively the comment may have been intended.

It's hardly unusual that a holiday finds various family members nursing old wounds or stewing about new disagreements. Take heart. The situation is reparable. Even the Hatfields and McCoys buried the hatchet eventually. You don't have to wait as long as they did to restore harmony to your family. A holiday represents a great opportunity to set things straight.

Whether the discord involves substantive matters or misunderstandings isn't paramount. What is vital is that someone in your family—you're as good a candidate as any—initiate a dialogue. If you've been at odds with a family member, propose a discussion. Get all the issues on the table and work through them as best you can. You may be a veteran of business sit-downs; this meeting will be more challenging because the emotional stakes are much higher.

Nevertheless, you may well find some common ground. Don't expect immediate rapprochement. It may take several discussions and some positive shared experiences to bring peace; holidays can be a great resource for those experiences. At the very least, you'll have begun a process that could help reunify your family. Holidays can be a time for healing; you'll do your family a great service by stepping into the role of mediator.

45.

Drop By When You Can

More than ever, we rely on modern communications tools to deliver our holiday best wishes. Greeting cards are perhaps the most obvious example, but there are many others. We take photos and mail them to family and friends. We create video memoirs with camcorders. We spread e-mail cheer to everyone listed in our electronic address books. Of course, no technological advance has supplanted the telephone as a means of keeping in touch. That's an impressive array of technology that we've developed to stay close to others, yet no form of indirect contact can approximate the warmth and satisfaction of in-person interaction.

Thus, one of the most important principles of holiday planning should be to maximize personal visits rather than falling back on indirect contact. You'll want to see as many friends and family as you can during the holiday, of course, but the post-holiday period can be an even more fertile period for "drop bys."

Planning for Christmas/Hanukkah can be so frenzied that no one has time for spontaneous visits. So how about that week between Christmas and New Year's Day? For many, the hustle and bustle is over, yet work schedules still may be relaxed. People are more relaxed, more receptive to unstructured time. This can be the best week of the year for dropping by.

Hop in the car and touch base with your friends. Invite them to your home to do the same. Think about your neighbors, as well. You may have checked on an elderly neighbor with a phone call before Christmas. Now is a great time to drop by. You'll see a big smile light up your neighbor's face. Useful as it is, e-mail never smiles.

46.
Those Who Work
While We Celebrate

We tend to think of holidays as universal, with everyone celebrating the same event at the same time. Yet in our complex society, a significant number of people work right through the holidays. In fact, if they didn't work, our holiday celebrations would be less enjoyable—and perhaps less secure.

Public safety officials are a key category of holiday workers. For many police and firefighters, holidays actually are a time of special vigilance because holiday travel brings with it the possibility of accidents. Hospital workers and paramedics also labor on holidays. If you or a loved one ever has needed emergency medical care on a holiday, you were pretty grateful to find that these fine folks were on the job rather than partying.

The media and entertainment sector is another that can't afford time off on holidays. We still watch the news on holidays, meaning that production crews and reporters must work to bring us that news. We expect to enjoy coverage of parades, sports contests, and other special events; where live TV is concerned, thousands of people must labor to bring us the images that we've come to regard as an integral part of holidays.

Show the true spirit of the holiday by remembering these folks with some small act of kindness. Take a tin of cookies to the nurses and doctors who were so available and effective when you needed them. Gather with some friends outside the police station and salute the officers with a carol. Your gesture need not be grand; if it's genuine, you'll create a special moment for those for whom every day is Labor Day.

47.

Many Traditions in One Family

The world observes its holidays in a broad variety of ways, celebrating with customs that are a product of culture, faith, and geography, to name only a few influences. When marriage brings several of those traditions together within a single family, the result can be enlightenment for all—or an ongoing source of tension that can threaten to split the family along religious or cultural lines.

Interfaith marriages are quite common these days; most people accept them as a matter of course and have little trouble welcoming the newcomers to the family. Yet holidays, with their cherished traditions and vivid symbols, raise the emotional stakes. If your family has celebrated around a Christmas tree for years, they may be distraught when you inform them that you're not erecting a tree this year out of respect for your spouse's beliefs. The reverse also is true. Your relatives may react viscerally when you inform them that you're displaying a tree this year to honor your spouse—even though your religion doesn't consider this a holiday.

In an interfaith marriage, perhaps the most important step to family harmony—as well as your own peace of mind—is for you and your spouse to reach agreement on how you will observe each key holiday. Discuss it regularly and openly. If your Christmas would be empty without a tree, let your spouse know that. On the other hand, if a tree would make you uncomfortable, advise your spouse of that. Develop the approach to decorating, worship, gifts, and entertainment that works best for both of you. Ideally, you'll come up with a protocol that pays homage to all of the beliefs and traditions each of you brings to the marriage.

When you have your model worked out, let other family members know what you have decided. Speak with them well in advance of the holidays, so that they'll have time to absorb and get comfortable with any new ideas. If you encounter resistance, do your best to explain to your loved ones that your new approach to the holiday is a way to blend your family's beliefs and customs. With your guidance, they'll soon understand that they, too, will be enriched by your multicultural celebration.

48.

When Is It Okay to Watch TV?

You're having a wonderful holiday. The entire family is there. Everyone's getting along famously for a change. Just when you think that you're about to get through the day without even the smallest skirmish, someone asks, "Mind if I turn on the Blue-Gray Game?" The fairy tale holiday goes up in smoke as the men gather around the tube while the ladies repair to the kitchen.

It's a classic holiday encounter that pits the rules of the house versus the pleasures of the guests. Whether you're hosting or a guest, these small conflicts can sour your holiday celebration if you let them.

What's called for here is a little diplomacy, a little give and take. Certain house rules probably should be inviolable. If, for example, you don't permit smoking in your house for health reasons, your guests should understand that in advance and be prepared to comply. This is a rule that pertains to health rather than manners, so it's not unreasonable to expect strict adherence.

Prohibiting television-watching, on the other hand, is more a rule of style and probably can be relaxed for this special occasion. Watching your family watch football might not be your holiday ideal, but they're all together and they're all enjoying each other's company; your holiday could be a lot worse.

You can apply the same approach when you're a guest. If the house rule is no smoking, don't push it. Step outside if you must smoke, and don't fuss over this small inconvenience. If the house rule is no scraps for the pets, resist the temptation to give Rusty that last piece of turkey skin. Remember, your host has imposed this rule for a reason. Even though you might not agree with the logic behind it, being willful and violating your host's policies would be needlessly rude.

When considering house rules, both hosts and guests should bring a little empathy to the table. When mutual understanding is on the menu, the meal will be an unqualified success.

49.

The Neighborhood Grinch

Every neighborhood has one: the man who darkens his house at Halloween because he doesn't want to be bothered with trick-or-treaters; the woman who grimaces and hurries away when you wish her a happy new year. Typically, we react to our neighborhood grouches in one of two ways. Either we ignore them, not wanting their gloomy spirits to spoil our holidays, or we try to impose our good cheer on them. Neither may be exactly the right approach.

Remember that your neighbors may resist holiday fellowship for a variety of reasons. Some may simply prefer solitude; in those cases, any outpouring of good will on your part likely will be met with stony silence, frustrating you in the process. Others may be suffering the loss of loved ones. For them, your joy may be an unbearable reminder of the pleasure that they don't expect to experience ever again.

Some of those that you typecast as grinches may not be feeling well, a situation that you would be hard-pressed to remedy. For others, the malaise may be driven by economic difficulties. Their seemingly sour disposition may be a strategy to discourage you from presenting them with gifts, since they lack the resources to respond in kind.

If you understand all of the possibilities, you might be able to creatively channel your natural inclination to spread holiday good will. You may not be able to reach someone, although it's hard to imagine even the most rugged individualist turning a deaf ear to carolers on the doorstep. To help those who may be ailing, a silent, unbidden favor—shoveling the snow from their front walk or driveway, for example—might help rekindle the holiday spirit.

If you know that your neighbors can't afford to purchase gifts, don't embarrass them with expensive presents. A handmade card from your kids or a plate of homemade cookies is a heartfelt but inexpensive way of bringing them into the holiday loop.

If your neighbors are lost in holidays past, drop by to talk to them about good times. Once they brighten up, you might find them receptive to an invitation to this year's party at your house. If you use the past as a lead-in to the present, you may find that your neighbor isn't such a grinch, after all.

50.

Financing Your Holidays

One of our most dubious holiday traditions is spending for the event beyond our means. Even the most careful shoppers tend to throw out the budget in the belief that holidays shouldn't follow any spending rules, and that they should purchase freely because that's part of the spirit of the season. When you approach holidays with unrestrained spending, though, the post-holiday season can feel bleak when you encounter credit card bills that you can't handle.

With just a little savvy planning, you can reduce the pressures of credit card debt and still have the holiday that you want. All it takes is a little creativity and discipline on both the saving and spending ends.

To help you build savings, tuck a little away each month for holiday spending. This was the principle behind the old "Christmas Club" program that banks used to offer: Deposit a small sum in a dedicated bank account each week or month, and withdraw it right before the holiday, with a little interest to boot. Unfortunately, the interest often was negligible. You can do better than that with some elementary savings vehicles.

For example, consider a six-month certificate of deposit. Not only will your money earn interest, but it will be locked up beyond your reach. You won't be able to access it, at least not without penalty, so you know that it will be there for you when the holiday approaches.

On the spending side, you can work some magic by thinking of gift-purchasing as a year-round assignment. If you see an item on sale in May that would make a great gift for a loved one, scoop it up then. Do this often enough, and your savings could be significant indeed.

It may seem odd at first to be making Christmas/Hanukkah purchases in the spring or summer, but doing so gives you the best of both worlds. You're sticking to a well-designed spending approach, yet you're yielding to impulse in selecting gifts. Call it "planned spontaneity," if you will—it can help insure that credit card bills won't erode your holiday joy.

51.

It's Okay to Cut Back

We often have a sense that each holiday must be more spectacular than the last. We want more people around the table than we entertained last year, more dishes to feed them, more decorations to enchant them, and more gifts to enthrall them. If this year's celebration isn't fancier than last year's, we fear that we're disappointing our children and our relatives. Our self-esteem can take a big hit, as a result.

If you view holidays as showcases for ever-more-uninhibited spending and display, you may have a fundamental flaw in your approach. Twinkling lights and expensive gifts are nice embellishments, but they're only that—embellishments. You and your loved ones are the main players. If you're all together for holidays, your affairs are automatically successful.

That's why it may be a mistake to view holidays as progressions from modest affairs to lavish extravaganzas. There will be those times when business has been good to you, leaving you with plenty of discretionary funds to spend on holiday decor and gifts. If that's how you want to spend your money, no one can dispute your choice. Splurging on the holiday will bring you satisfaction; that, after all, is what money *should* do.

However, you also may encounter holidays when an economic downturn, business reversals, or unexpected family expenses leave you in a financial bind. Just as you spend liberally on holidays when you're flush, now is the time to cut back and conserve for needs that may be more vital. Almost everyone experiences tough times; scaling back your holidays is a prudent way to cope.

Cut back when you need to, and don't stress about it. If you're with your loved ones, you'll have all the holiday you need. Anything beyond that is a bonus.

52.

You Keep the
Economy Humming

It's no secret that holiday sales can make or break many retailers. Candy purveyors, for example, depend inordinately on Easter and Halloween. Similarly, producers of consumer goods—particularly in the toys, electronics, and giftware sectors—count on Christmas/Hanukkah purchases for much of their annual sales. If holiday sales are down, there's simply no way for many retailers to make up the difference. They clear out their inventory with sales at deep discounts and chalk it up to a bad year.

Knowing that our holiday purchases are the linchpin of the retail sector is a thought at once ennobling and scary. It's gratifying because it makes us realize that each of us, lone consumers though we are, is contributing to the greater economic good. When we make our holiday purchases, we produce a beneficial ripple effect throughout the entire economy. Yet our role as an economic engine can be disconcerting, as well—if we cut back on our holiday spending, does that mean that we're hurting the economy and putting the jobs that depend on holiday sales in peril?

The heavy weight of the American economy is holiday pressure that you don't need and shouldn't shoulder. The discretionary income available to consumers for holiday spending rises and falls, but whether you're spending a lot or a little, the retail sector survives. What's most important is to stick to your plan and budget.

If you're able to spend a little more for a particular holiday, it's nice to know that you're a generous gift giver, as well as contributing to the greater economic good. However, when circumstances force you to reduce your spending, don't feel that you're letting your community down. Do what you need to do to make your holidays happy and affordable.

53.

Dealing with Disappointment

As we plan our holidays, we envision these special days unfolding without even the smallest glitch. As we live through our holidays, they often bring a measure of disappointment along with the expected pleasure.

Sometimes, the disappointment is valid. This happens when beloved family members can't be with us, or when injury or illness intrudes on the event. Here, we must work through our disappointment, because its causes are real, its impact unavoidable.

On other holidays, we invite disappointment with unrealistic expectations or by focusing on the wrong aspects of the event. You open a present, and find a gift you can't possibly use; it's the wrong size, the wrong color, and there's no accompanying exchange slip. Even worse, your kids open their gifts, and you don't see the bright smiles and squeals of glee that are sure signs that you've picked them a winner. Worse, they look positively shattered. This feeling—disappointment at your children's disappointment—may be the unhappiest holiday emotion of all.

When you find disappointment gnawing at you, step back and consider what's happening. You're allowing your evaluation of the holiday to be distorted by elements that may not be central to the celebration. So what if you can't use a particular gift? You received other presents that were more practical. Moreover, someone thought enough of you to buy you something special. That counts a whole lot more than the item itself.

As for your kids, they have other packages to open, as well. Once you explain the uses and value of the disappointing presents to them, or once they begin to use the gifts, you may find their disappointment turning to satisfaction and gratitude.

If you keep your focus on the main goals of your holiday, you'll take the edge off disappointment. When you're with your family and celebrating the holiday together, you have the key components of a wonderful event.

54.

Two or More Is a Celebration!

On holidays, we typically surround ourselves with as many family and friends as we can assemble. For many of us, family reunions are the principal goal and benefit of holidays. Any activities that we may plan when we're together aren't nearly as important as simply being together.

Yet there are those holidays when try as you might to gather everyone, your family remains scattered. Professional responsibilities or distance may be the reason. Everyone can't afford to come home for every holiday, so they must choose carefully—and this holiday won't work out.

It's easy in these situations to view the glass as half empty rather than half full and focus inordinately on your missing loved ones. Not only can this dim your holiday needlessly, but it's also a disservice to those family and friends who *are* with you. Let them be the focus of your celebration.

You can bring in the absentees by phone or Internet. Get a full report from them on how their holiday is going, and share with them complete details of your event. If they protest that they're running up your phone bill, advise them that sharing the holiday with them is well worth the cost, and keep right on conversing.

Once you've spent time with the absentees, turn your full attention again to those who are with you, and fret no more about the missing. You've incorporated them into your holiday in the best way available, while the rest of your family is there in the flesh to celebrate with you.

Of course it's not the same without the balance of your family—holiday observances never are exactly the same. Circumstances change, but whenever two or more of you are gathered, it's a celebration.

55.

Is This the Vacation
That You Want?

For many of us, holiday preparations are so involved and demanding that we just can't accomplish everything unless we find extra time somewhere. Some of us use every available moment during weeknights and weekends but still find that we can't do it all. So we put in for vacation days to give us the cushion that we need to complete our holiday preparations.

There's nothing inherently wrong with this. If burning a few vacation days helps assure that your holidays go as planned, that may be vacation time well used. However, what is the potential effect on you if you exhaust your vacation days, and then have none available when you're desperate for a midyear break? Picture yourself grinding away, week after week, month after month, without vacation days to give you and your family a much-needed respite. You may regret your decision to allocate vacation days to holidays that didn't need to be nearly so complicated.

If you've built up a rich vacation day account, this may not be a dilemma for you. You can use some vacation time for holiday planning and still have plenty left over for a nice break or excursion later on. If your vacation days are limited, though, you may want to decide how to allocate those days well in advance of the vacation signup period.

When you work hard—and who doesn't these days?—vacations are vital. You need that time away for something more relaxing than holiday planning, which tends to build pressure rather than release it. If you agree with that, here's a good rule of thumb: Consider a holiday celebration only so demanding that you can prepare for it and execute it in your regular off hours. You'll have a wonderful affair, and you'll avoid spending vacation days that you may sorely need later. Should you find that your holiday planning takes more time than anticipated, perhaps you can use a personal day in an emergency. If you follow this guideline, you'll have the holiday that you want now—and the vacation that you need later.

56.

The Importance
of Staying in Touch

As you review your card list each Christmas/Hanukkah season, you invariably come across the names of people that are no longer part of your daily commerce. Relocation may have put considerable distance between you and these people, or perhaps they still live in your region, but you find that your paths haven't crossed in some time. Does that mean that you should cross them off your list?

There's not much upside—and a whole lot of downside—to wielding the ax too aggressively. Yes, you save a card and a few dimes on postage, but you don't gain much other than that.

On the other hand, if you eliminate them, and they similarly remove you from their lists, you've severed what may be the last remaining link between you. Our lives are as rich as they are primarily because of our connections to so many people. We have our family circle, our work group, our neighbors, our gym buddies and more. Ties to friends brighten our lives. Seeing familiar faces makes us feel comfortable and gives our days an appealing steadiness.

Christmas cards serve much the same purpose. They let you know that your friends are out there, providing a comfort zone for your life with a network that can be reactivated whenever it makes sense to do so.

A better idea is to strengthen connections rather than terminate them. If you encounter a long-lost friend on your holiday card list, continue to send a card—and track down your old pal via phone or e-mail. If your friend remains local, make arrangements to get together soon. Your correspondents are out there, "sleeper agents" of friendship, waiting only for you to awaken them.

57.

Here's to the Holiday Heroes!

Every community depends on its unsung holiday heroes: the folks who establish angel trees to gather toys for needy kids; the organizations that collect canned foods to provide Thanksgiving dinners for the homeless; the groups that stage fireworks shows on Independence Day. In many cases, we take their selfless work for granted. This doesn't make us bad people, but perhaps we could be more attentive to those who help make the holidays bright.

For example, think about the last time that you and your kids ooohed and aaahed at a local fireworks display. Whose property did you watch from, and did you remember to thank them for their hospitality? Did you wonder for even a moment about what civic group was responsible for the fireworks and how much money they must need to stage such a memorable show each year?

A good resolution is to be more attentive to your holiday heroes. If you're able to contribute to angel tree or canned food drives, that's great! If you can volunteer to assist the effort, better still. However, if you can't make a financial or in-kind contribution, you still can express your appreciation. If your neighbors are hosting the community fireworks gathering, ask them if you can help clean up when the festivities are over. Find out which organization was responsible for the display, and then follow up by sending them a thank-you note. Better still, write a letter to the editor of your hometown newspaper. Your published thanks will have a much broader impact than a private note would.

It could be argued that the selfless volunteers who spread holiday joy reap plenty of satisfaction from a job well done. While this certainly is true, even holiday heroes need specific affirmation that their efforts are appreciated from time to time. You can provide that affirmation. When you do, you'll be encouraging your holiday heroes to press on for yet another year.

58.

The Meaning of the New Year

We tend to measure the most important aspects of our lives with twelve-month rulers. We count our time on earth in years. We evaluate the growth or decline in our investments in annual increments. We gauge our well-being in terms of the health and prosperity that we enjoyed during the year. Thus, as each year ends, we're prepared to label it a success or a failure based on the personal measures that each of us employs.

The media reinforces the notion of the year as yardstick by inundating us with a flurry of "top ten" or "top one hundred" lists—films, books, songs, news events. Creative works, it seems, must be cataloged and ranked by year's end if they're to be considered significant.

In some ways, using one year to evaluate ourselves is purely arbitrary. There's nothing sacred about the period between January 1 and December 31. We might just as profitably take stock every six months, or every two or three years, for that matter. The danger of using a year is that a period of just that length might distort your self-assessments. A disappointing year, for example, might have been preceded by five rewarding years, when you and your family enjoyed excellent health, and you reached your most cherished goals. In this case, your year-end review might discourage you when such a reaction is unwarranted.

For all that, year-to-year comparisons are as convenient as they are inevitable. So when you engage in your year-end review, remember to take the long view. Consider what you've accomplished or failed to achieve in the year just ending, but keep it in the proper perspective. How has your life been generally in the past few years—even the past decade? If it's been going well, you won't be overly concerned about the few speed bumps that you hit during the most recent twelve months.

Don't forget to look ahead, as well as back. It's true that a year is ending, but it's just as true that a new one is beginning. If you convert your experiences during the past year to plan of action for the next twelve months, you'll be ushering in a happy new year!

59.

When the Ball Drops

Watching the ball drop in Times Square each New Year's Eve may be the closest thing that we have to a national holiday experience. Despite our different faiths and philosophies, we settle in collectively to toast the new year and shout with joy when it arrives. Yet the emotions that we feel as the final seconds slip away may be mixed.

We know what the throngs gathered in Times Square are feeling. Theirs is an apparently unabashed enthusiasm for the immediate future, a joy unencumbered by any musings about the year just ending. They're ready to press on, excited about their personal future and the prospects for the world.

Others are given to more quiet reflection about the waning year. If they've gone through rough economic times or emotional crises during the year, they may be less likely to embrace the new year than they are to ponder the old one.

Most of us typically have a foot in both camps. We *are* looking forward to a healthy and happy new year even as we reminisce about the year gone by—and especially about loved ones no longer here to celebrate with us.

There's no need to feel guilty about conflicting feelings. A certain amount of ambivalence is to be expected at these watershed moments. It's natural to look both forward and backward as the ball begins its inevitable descent.

So if you catch yourself momentarily adrift on the sea of the past on New Year's Eve, that's okay. If you're anticipating the months ahead with only an occasional nod to the past, that's okay, too. Our lives are shaped by the events of the past and our visions for the future; it's no surprise that these forces meet, like old friends with unfinished business, each New Year's Eve.

60.

The Comfort of Ritual

When we trim the tree, color Easter eggs, or dress our kids in scary Halloween costumes, we're participating in rituals that have come to play an important role in our holidays. Viewed in isolation, few of these rituals seem integral to holidays. For example, our kids could go trick-or-treating without costumes and come away with the same candy haul. Christmas still would be Christmas without pine trees in our living rooms. Goodness knows, we could enjoy Easter without gorging on chocolate and jelly eggs.

Yet our holidays wouldn't be the same without rituals. Most holidays were designed to commemorate historic people and events, and these customs enhance the celebration. However, with the passage of time, we've come to identify the holidays more with the rituals and less with the historic people and events. For better or worse, ritual is the link between the holidays of yesterday and the celebrations of today.

As you outfit your kids for this year's trick-or-treating, you may remember your own Halloween experiences fondly. While you trim this year's tree with your family, you may be carried back many years to your childhood Christmas experiences, again feeling protected and warm as you did back then. That's the power of ritual.

Newer holidays that lack a rich tradition of rituals may not have the same hold on you. Think about Presidents' Day and Martin Luther King Jr. Day. These remembrances of men who were seminal figures in our history should be major events to all Americans, yet they seem to lack the force of other holidays. Perhaps it's because they have yet to develop the rituals that stamp them on our hearts and minds. (The annual Presidents' Day sale at the local discount department store, though it may feature bargains galore, doesn't count as an endearing ritual.)

As you plan your holidays, remember the key role that ritual plays. Ritual is an aspect of your celebrations that you may not want to modify unless absolutely necessary because ritual may provide the boundaries for your holiday comfort zone.

61.

Your Personal
Holiday Schedule

When you try to cram too much preparation into too little time, holiday stress will almost certainly result. You're busy enough with your work, family, and personal chores. Add holiday preparation to the list, and the load may become too burdensome.

One way to make your responsibilities more manageable is to list and organize them. Once you have your tasks documented, you can match them with the available windows in your schedule. This will maximize your efficiency and enable you to accomplish as much as possible.

Yet even the most adept holiday planners tend to focus so narrowly on family and friends that they forget their own needs. For example, you may want to splurge on a new Easter suit or dress, or you might need a visit to the salon. Perhaps your pets require grooming before the big day. These sundry tasks are personal rather than family-oriented, and they take time to accomplish. It's easy to overlook them, yet doing so may cause or aggravate holiday anxiety.

Here's a potential remedy. When you create your holiday to-do list, make sure you assign priority to these tasks as you would other important tasks. Budget time for them just as you do for decorating the house and purchasing gifts for the family. If they're important to your sense of fulfillment, they're important enough to become part of your holiday schedule.

If you don't get each of these tasks done, it's not the end of the world. Try to achieve a balance when considering your schedule of personal items. They should be important enough to land on your hit list, but not so vital that missing them will mar your holiday.

62.

When the Celebration's Over

Holidays, alas, don't go on forever. Soon after the last guests have departed, it's typically time for you to get back to the usual routine at work. Even if you love your job, there can be a stark contrast between the warmth and togetherness that you experienced during the holidays and the more impersonal environment of the office. Getting back to the grind will be that much more difficult for you if your job is indeed a grind.

The danger is that this sudden and dramatic transition can leave you distracted or depressed, neither of which is a desired outcome of holidays. To prevent this, it may be a good idea to build a sort of buffer between your holiday celebration and your return to work.

For example, if you must return to work the day after a holiday, you might plan for an afternoon celebration so that you'll have the evening to relax and prepare the proper mindset for the office the next day. You might not be looking forward to work, but you'll at least have some time to change gears.

If your holiday has been particularly demanding—perhaps you were in charge of an event for a huge group—you might even follow it up with a personal day or a vacation day to help you ease back into the work mode. A vacation day that recharges you after an intense holiday may be a vacation day well used. It also can be a benefit to your employer, who will be able to count on your usual alertness and professionalism when you return.

If you find that establishing transition space helps, you might apply a similar approach to vacations. Instead of hustling back to work only hours after your vacation ends, come home from your trip a day early. Use that extra day off to lounge around. While it may not appear that you're doing anything special, you'll actually be preparing to resume your career responsibilities with the proper attitude. That's easier to do when you're kicking back.

63.

When Friends and
Family Can't Make It

Holidays bring friends and families together—at least that's one of the outcomes that we envision. Sometimes, however, circumstances conspire to keep loved ones apart.

For example, your family may be scattered. Some members may be unable to make it back home due to travel difficulties or work schedules that won't accommodate days off. Illness may intrude, or you may find that a loved one is hospitalized for the holiday. The absence of key family members always threatens to dull your holiday celebration, yet there may be ways to creatively deal with these situations.

If your family members are halfway around the world, even your ingenuity won't bring you all together for the holiday. In such cases, you'll have to rely on communications with missing loved ones to make your holiday complete. However, if your friends and family remain within reasonable traveling distance, take holidays to them.

Let's say that illness has left a good friend housebound. You can pack up the car and drop in. Take food and gifts with you and have a small-scale celebration at your ailing friend's home. Your pal will find the visit uplifting—and perhaps as good a treatment as any medicine.

Does this holiday also find a family member in the hospital? Once you leave your friend's house, motor directly to the hospital to celebrate with your relative. Take such gifts and treats as are appropriate, always being mindful of hospital rules and any dietary restrictions that your loved one may be following. Get staff and other patients to join in to give your party a real holiday feel.

Now you're ready to return home to share the rest of the holiday with the balance of your family. It should be a particularly wonderful event, since you've found ways to include your absent family and friends. So what if you end up celebrating three times in three separate venues? Your determination and creativity have assured that everyone in your circle will enjoy the holiday. By acting so nobly, you've enriched your own holiday, as well.

64.

It Doesn't All Depend on You

If you're the principal holiday-maker for your family, you may be so determined to create a memorable event that you overload yourself. When you're fixated on your preparation schedule, momentum builds, and you're like a speeding train that has lost its brakes. No one can derail you as you lurch from task to task on the track to holiday perfection.

Laudable as it is to strive for the best holiday for your family, this go-it-alone approach can have adverse consequences. The most obvious result is that your obsession with preparation can keep you from enjoying the fruits of your labor. If you alone are responsible for preparing everything, it will be pretty hard for you to relax and appreciate your good work. When your tasks are finally completed, your nervous energy is spent, and you have no more work to do, you might feel a sort of emptiness rather than a well-deserved sense of satisfaction.

A more subtle consequence of going it alone is that you shut off opportunities for others to participate in holiday planning. When family members work with you in preparing meals and decorating, they share in the rewards of a job well done. If you don't give them that chance, they may feel purposeless and less willing to join in the actual festivities.

One of your most important jobs as the holiday manager is to delegate responsibility. You'll probably find a host of volunteers among your family. Accept their offers, if the tasks that they propose make sense. Where their specific chores don't seem helpful, politely steer them in more useful directions. They can help with cooking and cleanup, with transporting guests to and from the celebration and making sure that small children are occupied.

If volunteers aren't forthcoming, give some assignments. Don't be bashful about doling out work. Once your family and guests know that you're genuinely interested in their help, they'll join in enthusiastically.

A successful holiday doesn't all depend on you. In fact, if you make holiday planning as inclusive as possible, it's much more likely that your affair will be memorable for all.

65.

Avoiding Holiday Depression

Holidays are supposed to be a source of happiness and fulfillment. Yet if you feel anxious, overwhelmed, lonely, or inadequate each time a major holiday rolls around, you're not alone. Many people rank holiday anxiety right up there with job interviews—not a notorious source of happiness and fulfillment.

Why do so many of us suffer the "holiday blues"? The National Mental Health Association (NMHA) identifies "stress, fatigue, unrealistic expectations, over-commercialization, financial concerns, and the inability to be with one's family and friends" as the chief culprits. Further, notes the NMHA: "The demands of shopping, parties, family reunions, and house guests also contribute to feelings of tension. People who do not become depressed may develop other stress responses, such as: headaches, over-drinking, over-eating, and difficulty sleeping."

If your holiday depression is severe and chronic, you may want to seek professional help, but the NMHA also advises that self-help can help beat the holiday blues. Here are some ways to cope.

- Delegate some of your holiday management duties. "Save time for yourself!" the NMHA advises. "Let others share responsibility of activities."

- "Try something new. Celebrate the holidays in a new way."

- Remember that you can't do it all. "Try to set realistic goals for yourself," suggests the NMHA. "Pace yourself. Organize your time. Make a list and prioritize the important activities...."

- "Spend time with supportive and caring people. Reach out and make new friends or contact someone you haven't heard from for awhile."

- Develop a future orientation rather than pining for the holidays of yore. Says the NMHA: "Leave 'yesteryear' in the past and look toward the future....Don't set yourself up in comparing today with the 'good ol' days.'"

- "Do something for someone else. Try volunteering some time to help others."

Finally, if you're glum, remember that your melancholy might have rational, real-world causes that no holiday can eliminate. As the NMHA puts it, "...the holiday season does not banish reasons for feeling sad or lonely; there is room for these feelings in the present, even if the person chooses not to express them."

66.

Let the Sun Shine!

The winter holidays are nearing, and you're beginning to experience that familiar edginess. Knowing that you're supposed to be buoyed by the coming season of joy only intensifies your feelings of inadequacy. You have a classic case of the "holiday blues," right? Perhaps, but don't be too hasty with your diagnosis. The National Mental Health Association (NMHA) does encourage self-help as a way of coping with holiday blues, but you might be experiencing a variant that's more related to your environment.

This ailment is called seasonal affective disorder (SAD), and it results from fewer hours of sunlight as days grow shorter during the winter months. Because the most intense and demanding holidays fall during the winter, it's easy to mistake your moodiness for holiday anxiety, but if it's SAD that has you down, your condition may not exclusively be a product of the stresses of the season.

According to the NMHA, SAD is not fully understood but is thought to be related to melatonin, a sleep-related hormone secreted by the brain and produced at increased levels in the dark. Since we have less daylight in winter, we produce more melatonin. Symptoms of SAD—which pretty much mirror those of depression—include changes in eating and sleeping habits, anxiety, and loss of pleasure in activities once enjoyed. The major difference between SAD and depression is that the symptoms of SAD occur *only* in the colder months and are alleviated in the spring and summer. The NMHA estimates that six percent of all Americans suffer from SAD. Another ten to twenty percent may experience a milder form of SAD.

The happy news about SAD is that it responds to intervention—sometimes nothing more elaborate than a walk outdoors. Another approach is phototherapy, which involves a few hours of exposure to intense light. It's a convenient treatment, since SAD sufferers can bathe in brightness—often delivered by a device called a "light box"—as they perform their regular work or household activities.

So as the winter holidays approach, implement all of the common-sense measures recommended by the NMHA to ward off or cope with the blues. Keep your expectations realistic, share responsibility with others, spend time with empathetic people, and look ahead rather than back. If you continue to be troubled by sadness that can't be rationally explained, it might be time for consultation with a professional about SAD. It could be that once you get a little more sun, your holidays will be brighter—and your attitude and energy level generally will perk up, as well.

67.

The Inevitable Letdown

You've sung your last carol for the year, and your loved ones have scattered to their respective homes in far-flung cities. Your house is a cluttered mess that will need your attention before it's livable again. There's no doubt that the holiday is over.

It's natural at this moment to experience a little letdown. You've been on a "holiday high" for weeks now as you busily prepared for the event. You were organizing, executing, anticipating, and enjoying. Your mind was fully occupied for just about every waking moment. Now that it's all over, you have no immediate tasks at hand save housecleaning, so you may feel adrift or purposeless. Your temporary "low" is compounded by the absence of your family; you saw them all too briefly, and now they're gone again. You may have experienced something similar to this at work when you wrapped up a major project and felt temporarily empty, unable to muster up enough energy to be your usual productive self.

Don't be alarmed by this momentary lethargy. You've been at full throttle for so many weeks that your mind and body are working together to slow you down. Think of this as a period of replenishment or recharging. You'll be back to full speed soon, so this brief period of inactivity is no cause for concern.

If you feel too guilty about doing nothing, you might engage in some light planning. Consider the gifts that you received for the holiday. Where will you display or store them? What will you need to reposition or discard to make room for them? You could also go through a mental review of the celebration that just ended. What worked well, and what aspects might you change for next year's event? You can plan ahead, but don't worry yet about implementation.

You'll find yourself perking up in a matter of days, ready to tackle new challenges. Perhaps the best way to cope with the inevitable post-holiday letdown is to understand that it's coming. Its impact is more likely to be minor when it doesn't take you by surprise.

68.

Media Madness

When you see the little elves on TV tobogganing down snowy peaks on electric shavers; when one silhouette gives the other a diamond ring; when the Mistress of the Night appears on the screen to hawk Halloween ware—you know that a holiday can't be far behind. One of the surest signs of a holiday's approach is a sort of media frenzy that reminds us that it's time to begin our shopping.

From the retailers' point of view, this media madness makes a great deal of sense. The sooner that we purchase, the more that we're likely to purchase—and the sooner they'll have our money. There's nothing inherently wrong with this, except for the tendency of retailers to rush the season and instill in us the first trembling of panic. *It can't be the holiday yet! I'm not ready.* That knot in the pit of your stomach turns even tighter when you click on your favorite radio station and find it awash in seasonal music, many weeks before the holiday arrives.

Rest assured that it *isn't* the holiday yet, and there's no reason for you to be ready. Paying attention to the hoopla can be a good thing, if you think of it as an early reminder to activate your holiday game plan. Premature advertisements may even help you to identify gifts for the people on your list.

However, the media blitz also can be a major contributor to holiday stress, should you take the messages too literally. If you approach each holiday with a plan and a schedule, you'll accomplish all of your goals without feeling the pressure that constant advertisements can create. Stick to your plan and schedule, and you'll be able to enjoy your preparations; getting ready, after all, should be among the greatest pleasures of any holiday, bringing with it the anticipation of the celebration to come. If you're confident of your plan, you'll be able to enjoy holiday advertisements without feeling anxious—a big plus right there.

69.

To Resolve or Not to Resolve?

The making of resolutions for the new year has become a tradition that most of us greet with a certain ambivalence. We look forward to developing—and sticking to—behavioral guidelines that will improve us as people. Yet our experience with failed resolutions might cause us to dread the coming of the new year, knowing that we may be headed for another boom-bust cycle of shiny new hopes followed by predictable failures.

To resolve or not to resolve? That is the question, but the answer isn't so simply stated. Our thinking on resolutions may be further complicated by the pressure that we feel from friends. Once we hear them discussing their resolve to quit smoking, to lose weight, or to work out regularly, we may want to jump on the resolution bandwagon—even though it's not clear in our own minds if these resolutions will work for us. Peer pressure only intensifies the resolution dilemma.

Perhaps a good approach to resolutions is to carefully consider those aspects of your behavior that may be modifiable. If it appears that a resolution will help you achieve a desired new behavior or outcome, then resolve to resolve. Make your resolution as specific and goal-oriented as possible. For example, when you say, "I resolve to lose weight," your goal is so vast, so vague, that you may not be able to develop the right game plan to accomplish it. It might be better to ground your resolution in specifics—"I resolve to lose ten pounds by Easter." Now you have a better idea of the steps of action that you must take to realize your objective.

Be mindful of your past failures, but don't let them inhibit your new improvement efforts. It's a new year and a new you. Everything is possible.

Then again, if you don't think that a resolution will help, don't succumb to pressure to make one. Nothing is as certain of failure as a half-hearted effort—which you're likely to give if your resolution is a product of peer pressure. If you're without resolutions this year, that's okay. You can resolve to help your friends stick to their resolutions.

70.

Write It Down

When your New Year's resolution remains an unwritten concept, it may be too elusive to have much force. Documenting an idea increases its power, outlining it for all to see.

Changing behavior is difficult, especially so when you're trying to reverse habits that have been years in the making. That's what resolutions usually address. You're much more likely to succeed if your resolutions are written.

Write them down—and don't squirrel them away in a notebook that you may toss aside and never open again. Post them on the wall where you, your family, and friends can see them. When you know that others are aware of your goals, you may strive even harder to achieve them.

When you achieve a milestone, don't forget to reward yourself. Splurge on a CD by your favorite artist, or get some friends to treat you to a movie. If your buddies are familiar with your progress, they'll be happy to oblige. That's the power of written resolutions.

71.

Your Yearly Game Plan

When we develop a corporate or personal budget, we typically include plenty of details, interim goals, and milestones. We know what we have to spend each quarter, we know what we want to achieve in each facet of our operations, and we frequently build in incentives for outstanding performance. We would never think of a budget that consisted of a single sentence: Expenditures will not exceed revenues.

Why is it, then, that we style our New Year's resolutions in single sentences—*I will lose weight,* or *I will exercise more*—without including any of the benchmarks or details that we include in financial budgets? Perhaps it's because we're not accustomed to thinking of behavior in the same way as we regard budgets, dense as they are with categories and figures. Yet we might have much more success with resolutions if we regarded them as systematic plans rather than as laudable but gauzy ideals.

If you have a group of behavioral goals that you would like to achieve, try treating them as you would a budget. Give each one a separate page in a notebook or ledger, or create a separate document for each if you're crafting your behavioral plan on a computer. On each page, begin with your ultimate objective for each resolution—the number of pounds that you'd like to lose, the number of workouts that you'd like to implement per week, and so on.

Now, build in some realistic timelines. Do you think that you can accomplish a five-pound weight loss the first month? Record that as your first interim goal. As you get into the swing of your diet, do you expect to increase the pace of your weight loss? Document that in your yearly plan, as well.

Don't forget to incorporate changes in routine that you know will affect your progress. For example, if you have a week-long business trip coming up this spring, you're well aware that time away can wreak havoc with your exercise schedule. Make a note on your plan to explore—well in advance—hotels in your destination city that offer gyms or swimming pools so that you can stay on track for your exercise goal.

Accomplishing financial goals is tough, but achieving behavioral objectives is no less challenging. In each case, a well-conceived plan will help you succeed. Failure, on the other hand, never needs a plan.

72.

...For Tomorrow We Diet

How many times do you hear people say, even as they wolf down another slice of Christmas nut roll, "It's okay, because I'm starting a diet right after the holiday?" You greet the remark with public encouragement but private skepticism, considering it a stall tactic. Then you realize rather sheepishly that it's the same procrastination you've engaged in a time or two before.

We seem to satisfy some deep psychological need when we justify holiday indulgence by pledging to atone for it beginning the very next day or next week. However, this is a lose-lose situation. If you aren't really serious about beginning a program to modify some aspect of your behavior, you may view yourself as a failure right out of the box. You also run the risk that others will see you that way, and that won't do much good for your self-esteem.

Yet if you do resolve to diet, quit smoking, or exercise more after the holiday, and you mean what you say, your enjoyment of the holiday may become a casualty. In addition, you know that you're making your behavior modification program even tougher by overindulging during the holiday.

If you aren't seriously determined to improve your behavior in a key area after the holiday, don't suggest—to yourself or anyone else—that you are. Celebrate to the extent that you see fit. When you're ready for a change, you can approach it with care rather than a casual remark that gets you nowhere.

However, if you're serious about behavior modification, begin it now, before the holiday. If you're planning to diet, do some preliminary research. Talk to a nutritionist about the best diet for you. Surf the Web to identify an exercise schedule that will complement your diet.

When you do some of the prep work now, you'll be demonstrating to yourself just how serious you are about this resolution thing. You can enjoy the holiday knowing that you already have your improvement program in the works.

73.

Mutual Support
Goes a Long Way

New Year's resolutions seem harmless enough. If you stick to them, you improve your behavior in important and desirable ways. If you break them, you're no worse off than you were before— or are you? There may be a joker in the resolutions deck—the impact of failure on your self-image.

When you don't achieve your goals, you may come to view yourself as something less than an effective agent in your own life. You may shun responsibility because in your heart of hearts, you don't think that you can measure up. You can even come to accept failure more readily than you should, since that's what you've always experienced in the past.

Does that mean that you should avoid resolutions? Not at all. Modifying certain unwanted aspects of your behavioral makeup can be a worthy goal. It does mean, however, that to achieve this goal, you may need a little help.

Support from others will go a long way to helping you keep your resolutions, while you, in turn, can extend similar assistance to those who are helping you. You can even form a "resolutions support group" with your friends. At the initial meeting, each of you can outline your goals and the specific steps that you'll take to get there. You can review everyone's plans, modify them, and work out a schedule of incentives to reward progress.

You can convene regularly to review the status of each group member—and to analyze any setbacks that have taken place. Since all of you will be experiencing similar challenges, no one is likely to render hasty or hurtful judgments. Moreover, advice offered by group members will be more credible than counsel from someone who isn't taking the same path.

Make sure that every member of your group has the key contact information—phone numbers and e-mail addresses—for all other participants. That way, you can reach out for assistance—and provide the same—at moments when resolve is wavering.

74.

Falling Off the
Resolution Wagon

Progress along the way to behavior modification can be uneven. We take two steps forward, one step backward, grit our teeth, and keep marching ahead. We keep marching ahead, that is, if we don't get discouraged and give up the quest any time that we fall off the resolution wagon.

Small setbacks are just about inevitable. Think back to the important goals that you've achieved and how difficult it was to achieve them. Did you successfully woo your spouse with one date? More likely, it took a series of encounters and a few misunderstandings before you knew what a great match you two would make.

How about your position at work? Did you arrive where you are through a single promotion? Or did it take years of hard labor—and possibly some frustrations when others were named to posts that you coveted while you were assigned less prestigious tasks? However, you persevered, and you got there.

If you apply these lessons to your New Year's resolutions, you'll realize that you won't be traveling in straight-line motion—you will encounter bumps or even detours along the way. Rather than throwing in the towel when you suffer a setback, you might want to analyze your failure.

If you sneaked a cigarette, was it because a friend smoked in your presence and you found the aroma irresistible? Was it because you dined in a restaurant that lacked a nonsmoking section, making the temptation of passive fumes unavoidable? If these were the phenomena that helped push you over the edge, you know now that you need to avoid these stimuli until your resolve is greater.

Take the same approach with dieting. If walking past the neighborhood bakery and its luscious confections in the window makes you backslide into a cheese Danish, change your route for now. Someday, you'll stroll proudly past that sweet shop without giving it a second glance. When that happens, you'll know that you've made it.

75.

How Hearty Should You Party?

Parties are a chance to be with friends and loosen up. They are one of the best features of holidays. Yet odd as it may seem, too many parties can aggravate holiday tensions rather than reduce them.

Once the party invitations roll in, they can have a way of piling up and throwing a monkey wrench into your well-planned schedule. There's the office party, of course—a second one if your spouse's company throws a bash—and perhaps a little departmental soiree, as well. A couple of your clients are having receptions; clearly it's good business to attend those. Your neighbor across the street throws an annual Christmas bash, and your absence would be conspicuous. The fitness center where you work out hosts a gala, and you certainly don't want to miss your sister-in-law's annual function, at least not if you want to preserve family harmony.

You never knew that you were so popular! It's gratifying to be on so many invitation lists, but do you have the time for so many parties? If holiday events start to intrude on the time that you've set aside for your own preparations, it can create conflicts for you—and pressure that the very parties themselves are supposed to relieve.

Should you have young children at home, a heavy social schedule can bring another complication—someone has to watch your kids while you're out. The need to find baby-sitters can be yet another worrisome element that you don't need.

One approach is to accept all of your holiday party invitations but cut your stays short. This won't lick the baby-sitter challenge, but all of your hosts will feel good when you show up—however briefly. You won't hurt their feelings or suffer subsequent guilt pangs.

You also can avoid party-induced tension by getting a good handle on your holiday objectives. What are your most important goals in preparing for the holiday? If you prioritize those, you'll know what time you can allocate to the party scene. You may find that you attend fewer events but enjoy them more because you're not fretting about the time that you're spending there. In other words, party as hearty as your schedule will allow.

76.

When Your Heart Is Heavy

One of the most challenging holiday obligations is to join in the festivities when you're in the throes of melancholy. Unfortunately, in the course of our lives, this happens more often than we'd care to acknowledge. Perhaps you've lost a family member or a good friend. You may be ailing yourself. Maybe it's something less severe, such as problems at work or in a relationship. These conditions may not be as dark as the absence or death of an intimate, but your heart may be heavy just the same.

When you're glum, the excitement of holidays may be the furthest thing from your mind, but come the holidays will, whether or not you're emotionally prepared for them. How should you address holidays in these circumstances? The conventional wisdom is that you should put aside your woes and participate as fully as you always do. You'll find, according to this theory, that you'll forget about your sadness, and that when the celebrations are over, you'll feel a whole lot better about yourself. Indeed, the fellowship that you feel at holidays may snap you out of your malaise.

At other times, though, you may find that solitude is your most urgent need. On those occasions, it's okay to gently beg off your friends' party invitations and hang back until you feel more like yourself.

If you're the principal holiday planner for your family, you may want to ask for help—or even pass the baton while you work through your sorrow. Others will understand your choice; most people have been through dark emotional times and know exactly what you're feeling.

Whether you decide to suspend your sadness and party or spend your holiday in quiet, solitary reflection, don't feel guilty about your course of action. You're not a party-pooper, and you're not indulging in self-pity. You've made the best choice for you in your current circumstances.

77.

For the Folks Who
Make Life Easier

Around the Christmas/Hanukkah holidays, we typically agonize over how to recognize the folks who make our lives easier. This group usually includes trash collectors, as well as postal and newspaper carriers. You also may wonder about appropriate gifts for your gardener, your baby-sitter, your barber or beautician—even your plumber, if he has just repaired a nasty leak that threatened to deep-six your holiday.

We ask ourselves the same questions each year: Is a card enough to express our appreciation? How can we send them cards when we don't know their full names, much less their addresses? If cash is better, how much is enough? Can municipal employees even accept cash gifts? With so many things to ponder, we may create a situation that's more stressful than it needs to be.

A good starting point is to remember that recognition should be a year-round objective. If you frequently convey appreciation to the folks who help you, what you do for the holidays becomes less critical.

Another good idea is to personalize these relationships as much as possible. If you're embarrassed because you don't know your postal carrier's name, now is a great time to stick out your hand, formally introduce yourself, and kick off an enduring friendship. When you spend a few minutes each day chatting with your postal carrier about the things important in both your lives, you'll be expressing your regard in ways that a holiday gift never could.

Finally, remember that every gift is appropriate, so long as it's thoughtful and heartfelt. Give some consideration to how you would like to say thanks. Once you do that, the monetary value of the gift is secondary.

If you're worried about giving cash to a government worker, why not send a letter to your trash collector's supervisor indicating how great your service has been? That could contribute to a promotion—and many happy holidays down the road.

78.

Great Expectations

We expect great things of holidays, counting on them to deliver warmth, fellowship, contentment—and those new kitchen gadgets that we've been hinting about for months. However, when we're dealing with family and friends whose expectations differ from ours, we may be setting ourselves up for a letdown. Some disappointments are minor and easily overcome, while others may be so deep that they imperil our holiday enjoyment, to say nothing of our equilibrium.

You've probably experienced a Mother's Day or a Father's Day when you were secretly hoping that your family presented you with a gift certificate to the new health club in town so that you could indulge in a comforting massage. Instead, the dears gave you breakfast in bed—and a nice mess to clean when they finally permitted you to arise.

Perhaps you were expecting to spend a romantic Valentine's Day with your beloved at an intimate resort by the bay. Instead, your better half proudly announced the acquisition of two tickets to spring training, which would be the site of your holiday getaway.

These disappointments typically are as temporary as they are common. Once you get over the immediate disappointment of receiving gifts that you don't want, you realize that your loved ones were, in their own way, doing something special for you. That's the best gift, and it's never disappointing.

What about a situation where your in-laws insist that they host the holiday gathering this year, in effect supplanting you as the perennial host? Are they making some adverse comment about the way that you executed your responsibilities, or trying to pull off a coup within the family? The answer probably is far less sinister, yet your bruised feelings may lead you to magnify the incident.

One way to keep your expectations realistic is to engage in regular communication with your family about the ways that holidays will be observed. If they know what you expect, and you in turn are familiar with their wishes, there's much less chance of a damaging misunderstanding.

It's also a good idea to keep your expectations realistic, knowing that compromise is inevitable when you're trying to match your hopes with the preferences of others. Aim high, and strive for the most satisfying holidays possible, but temper your expectations with the understanding that some things just won't work out as planned.

79.

Suspending Disbelief

Generally, a little skepticism is a good thing—it makes us less vulnerable to schemes and scams that may exploit us. However, if we yield to it, excessive skepticism can spoil holidays.

We're all probably a little cautious about the number of new holidays that seem to spring up overnight. If we're supervisors, we find that we're expected to honor our staff on Secretaries' Day. They, on the other hand, must return the favor on National Boss Day. Then management and labor both pitch in for Take Your Daughters to Work Day.

The most hard-boiled among us suspect that these holidays, and others of their ilk, have been contrived by the greeting card industry and other merchandisers to induce us to purchase their wares on these "special" days. However, if you delve into the history of most holidays, you'll find that their origins are genuine enough.

Both Mother's Day and Father's Day, for example, began as the tributes of individuals to their parents; local observances found a willing national audience, because the sentiment expressed was real and common to millions. Labor Day has its roots in a late-nineteenth-century parade to honor organized labor. Halloween dates back many centuries—well before the founding of any greeting card company. Of course, the origins of such major holidays as Christmas, Hanukkah, and Kwanzaa are well known and above reproach.

However, let's assume the worst case—that the slew of neo-holidays is the result of a conspiracy of retailers. Even if that's true, is it harmful to show just how much you appreciate your secretary or your boss on their special days? You know the answer to that. It's always a great idea to express appreciation, no matter how artificial the occasion may appear to you.

So don't abandon your skepticism—you'll continue to need a healthy dose of it in our modern world. Where holidays are concerned, though, suspend your disbelief and join in. Consider yourself a willing victim of the conspiracy to force holiday enjoyment upon you.

80.

Remember Your Pets!

Your pets can be a wonderful part of your holiday, but if you're a veteran pet person, you're well aware of how disruptive the little guys can be. When you get excited about holidays, they get excited about holidays; when they get excited, bad things happen. They get into the holiday turkey, munch on ornaments that have been in your family for years, or even take down the whole tree in their frenzied play.

What's the best way to ensure that pets and holidays mesh? A good approach is to make as few changes in the critters' routines as possible. Domestic animals tend to be creatures of habit. They may respond to changes with curiosity or fear, neither of which is likely to yield the type of behavior that you want from them on a busy holiday. This will be especially true on Independence Day, when the day-long noise from fireworks can drive them to extremes of uncharacteristic—and undesirable—behavior. When the bombs are bursting in midair, they'll need your utmost attention.

In extreme circumstances, you may have to quarantine your pets during the holiday party. This will be necessary if they don't respond well to crowds, or if one of your guests fears all animals—or yours in particular. Barring these extreme circumstances, stick with the routine. Feed your pets when and where they're usually fed, and walk them when and where they're usually walked. They'll usually repay you with their best behavior when they're not confronted by too many changes. If you have rules for your pets—no hand-fed human snacks, for example—make sure you familiarize your guests with your wishes.

Finally, involve your pets in the spirit of the holidays. Add colorful bandannas and collars to their usual attire. Present them with their own gifts. These need not be expensive. When your pets are full-fledged participants in the holiday, they'll know that they're loved, and they'll return that affection to you—a priceless holiday gift.

81.

Budgeting for Holidays

For most of us, "holiday budget" is an ugly contradiction in terms. We want our holidays to be merry and spontaneous, not driven by a restrictive spending plan. When we see a neat item that we know a loved one would like, we want to buy it and not worry about the cost. Credit cards have made impulse holidays more possible than ever before. We're able to purchase what we want and not worry about payments until long after the holiday has ended.

Think of the tradeoff here—a brief period of pleasure financed by many weeks or months of worrying about bill payments and cutting back in key areas to come up with the money to finance those spur-of-the-moment splurges. Perhaps a better approach is to develop a holiday budget that provides for ecstasy now—and no agony later.

Your budget need not be terribly formal. Take a notepad and jot down the key categories of holiday spending. "Gifts" are likely to be the most costly category. Include presents for your family, as well as those you'll be distributing at the office—and charitable contributions. You'll need a category for "entertainment," an important item if you're hosting the family gathering. Include the costs for all food and beverages; if you're planning a catered affair, your expenses in this category may rise appreciably.

"Travel" will be an item in some holiday budgets, and don't forget "cards." This may turn out to be the least expensive of your categories, but it's certainly significant enough to include.

When you have all of your categories, pencil in a dollar amount for each, add the numbers, and you'll have your preliminary holiday budget. Now, check it against the resources that you think you'll have available without taking on additional debt. If the figures match, you'll pretty much have the financing challenge of the holidays whipped. If you have more resources than you think you'll need, you're well-positioned to spring for some extras.

If your preliminary budget expenses exceed your projected resources, don't despair. Work on your budget a little to make it fit your financial capabilities.

When your budget is finalized, you're ready to hit the mall—or catalogs, or the Internet, whichever shopping mode you prefer. You can be as spontaneous as you like, as long as you stay within the overall confines of your budget. You'll have the holiday you want—and no bills to beset you in the months that follow. That's a great gift to bestow on yourself.

82.

Champagne on a Beer Budget

Some years will be so successful that you can afford all of the nice holiday touches that you would like. You can splurge on ornate and costly decorations, buy as many gifts as the trunk of your car can hold, and even work some expensive travel into your holiday celebration. No need to stick to a holiday budget in these prosperous times.

Other holidays, though, will find you short on cash, or with so many pressing financial obligations that you can't allocate much to holiday spending. It's not the circumstances that you would prefer, but limited funds need not diminish your enjoyment of any holiday. If you get creative, you can have champagne on a beer budget.

A good first step is to determine which of your holiday traditions are inviolable and which can be scaled back. Decorating usually is a fertile area for cutbacks. True, you may be used to scouring specialty shops and department stores for deep discounts on holiday trappings, but with a little discipline, you can resist those this year. Besides, your garage and attic are packed full of holiday paraphernalia that will serve you very well.

Here's where the creativity comes in. Assign each member of your family the task of making a holiday decoration from scratch. Costs for materials will be minimal, you'll end up with decorations that are conversation pieces, and your family will grow even closer through this common experience.

Take the same initiative with gifts, usually the most expensive element of holiday celebrations. Impose a limit on the number of gifts that each family member can purchase or receive. There may be some grumbling at first, but when your loved ones get more deeply into the chore, they'll realize that they must devote more time and effort to their gift selections than ever before. They can't make up in quantity what their gifts may lack in quality.

You may find that these measures, though inspired by tight funds, work so well that you'll want to employ them even when money is a little looser. They'll serve to involve your family in holiday planning in new and innovative ways, plus you'll be creating traditions that can be passed down through generations.

83.

You Say It's Your Birthday

Most of us anticipate and appreciate holidays throughout our lives. Kids, teens, adults, seniors—no matter where we are on the continuum, we bring the same enthusiasm to holidays.

Birthdays may be the most notorious exception. It's amazing how our attitude about birthdays—our most personal holidays, after all—changes through the course of our lives. When we're young, birthdays mean cake and presents, and they signal that we're a year closer to the things that we really want to do, such as drive and stay up late.

As we age, birthdays become more cautionary. We still can expect gifts from those closest to us, we still get together with friends and family to celebrate, but the celebrations may have a dark undertone—the years are slipping by. If ever we think that we might escape birthdays unscathed, some joker sends us a card announcing that we've reached The Big Five-Oh. As if we weren't keenly aware of it! It's during this midlife period that some people conceal their ages or even shave a few years where they think they can get by with that little white lie.

As seniors, we seem to regain our pride in who we are and what we've experienced. We disclose our age to anyone who'll listen. We've lived many years, and we're delighted when people know that we've endured and survived.

Seniors have it right. There's never a good reason to stop celebrating or acknowledging your birthday. When that day arrives, it's an important indication that you've thrived for another year, and that you're looking forward to many more. If you tiptoe around your birthday as if to deny that it's happening, you miss out on one of the more important celebrations of your life—one that symbolizes your perseverance and success.

Treat each birthday as you used to when you were young. Celebrate unabashedly. If it means yet another candle on the cake, so what? Congratulate yourself, take a deep breath, and blow.

84.

Keep Birthdays Special

Here's a holiday homily with which everyone born on December 26 or January 2 will agree: Birthdays need to be special and separate from holiday celebrations. When people have holiday babies in the family, there's a strong tendency to integrate birthday celebrations in their holiday affairs. By their very nature, holidays are stressful, bringing pressure that people tend to aggravate by wanting to do too much. Even a small-scale birthday party after a full-blown holiday affair may be more than we can cope with.

Then there's the financial component. Overdoing holidays can leave you broke for now—and with even less later when the credit card bills come rolling in. Thus, you may be tempted to designate something that you've already purchased for the holidays as the "birthday gift," canceling the need for still another costly trip to the mall.

For those of us of a certain age, this appears a sensible plan. We've all been short of money and energy after holiday celebrations, so we appreciate the attempt to honor our birthdays without additional stress and strain. However, children who are just developing a sense of self may misunderstand this pragmatic approach and begin to consider themselves as less than worthy. Their disappointment may deepen as they hear about the birthday parties of their contemporaries—those who weren't born around holidays—and find that their own celebrations pale by comparison.

Where children are involved, it's important to keep birthdays special. Present gifts at a time that's distinct from your holiday affair. Give them birthday cards not tied to the holiday, and wherever possible, stage a separate celebration for them. It can be a low-key affair—perhaps dinner at a special restaurant with your kids and a few of their friends. Whatever the format, you'll be reminding your kids that they're special to you. There's less risk that they'll view their birthdays as holiday afterthoughts.

85.

Suspending Household Rules

It's the holiday celebration that you dreamed of. Everything is going just right, when all of a sudden, your uncle lights up one of those foul-smelling cigars. Your brother's son takes the dog for a walk, then tramples over the carpet with muddy shoes. Your mother cranks up her favorite holiday album so loud that conversation becomes impossible. All of this at your house, where everyone knows your rules.

You can let these family scofflaws ruin your holiday, or you can step back, breathe deeply, and understand that some household rules simply must be suspended when large families are gathered. If you're cool on rules, you may find that some remedial action is possible. There's not much to do about the muddy carpet except remember to vacuum later. However, your uncle probably won't be offended if you remind him that cigar smoke bothers others and he needs to smoke outside. As for Mom, let her enjoy her music for awhile, and then gently ask if you can turn down the volume a bit. If your touch is deft, you'll be able to restore order without offending anyone.

The key to your peace of mind when you're the holiday host is to differentiate the critical rules from those that are more a matter of convenience. Where health is concerned, it's reasonable to insist on strict adherence to the rules. Dirt and clutter, on the other hand, can be addressed after the celebration is over. You'll be cleaning anyway, so another chore on the post-holiday list won't increase your burden much.

Make sure your guests know which are the immutable laws of your household—they'll probably be only too happy to obey. As for your other rules, be prepared to relax them for this special occasion. Your guests will appreciate your flexibility, and you'll relieve yourself of the pressures of having to enforce the unenforceable.

86.

Forget About the Joneses

Holidays never should be competitive—that is, you shouldn't judge your celebrations by how others conduct their events. However, because some aspects of holidays are quite visible, comparisons may be unavoidable.

Decorations invite easy comparisons. You and your family work hard to set Santa and his reindeer on your lawn—you even have a bright red bulb for Rudolph's nose. You stand back to admire your handiwork, when all of a sudden, you're blinded by the lights from the neighbors' display. They've illuminated every conceivable nook and cranny of their property. Your pride in your accomplishments suffers a serious blow, courtesy of your neighbors.

Other comparisons are more subtle—and therefore more insidious. Some of these begin with your kids, who invariably compare their holiday "take" with that of their friends. Try as they might to be good soldiers, your children eventually blurt it out: Others got better gifts than they did. You might be able to deal with your own disappointment, but having to bear the guilt of your kids' disappointment takes the feeling to another level.

While comparisons may be inevitable, they won't be hurtful if you keep your principal holiday objectives in mind. If your intention is to bring your family together and infuse the gathering with love— and you achieve that—then what your neighbor does shouldn't make any difference. If your goal is to volunteer with a community organization—and you do that—then who cares if someone else donated $100,000 to that group? You've created the best holiday for you, your family, and your community. No one could ask more of you.

So if the Joneses appear to outdo you in wattage or the price tags of their gifts, tip your cap without feeling envious or diminished. You're keeping up with your own holiday objectives. That's what matters most.

87.

The Role of Nostalgia

It would be hard to imagine a holiday today that doesn't trigger memories of holidays past. As you gather with your loved ones, you remember the Christmas of the big snowstorm, the Easter when the kids finally were old enough to participate in the community egg hunt, or the Veterans Day when your alma mater's band marched in the parade. All are warm memories that make your appreciation of today's holidays that much sharper.

If it serves as a link to pleasant memories, nostalgia is a welcome visitor at holiday functions. Yet there's also danger lurking in the past. When your current situation compares unfavorably to the circumstances that you used to enjoy, you may want to escape the present and opt for a prolonged stay in the past. You want to learn from your memories and experiences, of course, but you don't want to dwell in the past for an extended period.

By our nature, humans are time travelers. We operate in a present that's informed by the past and anticipates the future. This ability—perhaps it's even a necessity—to operate in all three of life's time zones is what distinguishes us from earth's other creatures. A life lived too much in the past, present, or future may not be a life fully lived.

So if your holidays don't seem entirely what they used to be, don't yield to the siren's song of nostalgia—at least not completely. Let those memories guide you in your creation of holidays now that bring you and your loved ones the same measure of fulfillment that you once experienced. If the Veterans Day parade excited you when you were young, take your kids or grandkids to this year's parade. If your children are grown and too old for the Easter egg hunt, collaborate with a nonprofit organization to treat some deserving youngsters to the party this year.

Nostalgia plays an important role in holidays, but not the primary role. You can take the initiative to make your current holidays rewarding—for you and for all those with whom you connect. Then you'll be creating holidays that themselves will be the stuff of nostalgia.

88.

Reach Out to the Community

According to Russian legend, the three wise men needed food and shelter during the search for the infant Jesus. They approached a woman named Babouschka for help, only to be turned away. As we all know, their journey ultimately was a success, but Babouschka wasn't so lucky. Stricken by guilt over her uncharitable conduct, she now roams the Russian countryside, searching for Christ and distributing gifts to children along the way.

As with so many of our holiday tales, the Babouschka story is an allegory with a moral for us—that we should assist those in need whenever the opportunity arises. We can also create those opportunities ourselves. Christmas may be the best occasion for good deeds, because so many civic and charitable organizations are at their most active then. Yet many other holidays can serve as platforms for public service.

Here are some ideas for holiday helpfulness. Don't limit yourself to these. With a little ingenuity, you'll do as much good as the repentant Babouschka.

- On Memorial Day, is the grave of a valiant soldier choked with weeds? Trim the site, and say a silent thank you. Visit a veterans' hospital. (This also is a fine idea for Veterans Day.) You can help serve meals, volunteer at bingo and other organized events, or just chat with residents. All are contributions that will be appreciated.

- On Mother's Day or Father's Day, some kids in your community may not have the opportunity to celebrate these holidays—for obvious reasons. Investigate what it would take to become a Big Brother or Big Sister to these youngsters.

- On Groundhog Day, check with a local pet shelter and see what the animals in your community most need.

- On Labor Day, employers have many creative options for recognizing the outstanding performance of workers. One would be to initiate a scholarship fund for which only the children of employees would be eligible.

89.

The "Crèche-Mess" Season

Harbingers of Christmas/Hanukkah are everywhere—an agreeable chill in the air, your favorite music on the radio, and communities split over the best way to stage a seasonal display without violating the rights of those who don't observe these holidays.

It's a struggle that's become as predictable as Santa's schedule. Some municipal official proposes the erection of a crèche or other nativity scene at the town hall, a civil libertarian expresses opposition to this seeming blending of church and state, and the battle is on. Typically, media coverage of the dispute only encourages both sides to dig in. Once positions harden, you can forget about peace in town, much less peace on earth.

How sad it is that this type of dispute can dim the holiday spirit for an entire community! Yet if you find yourself a participant in, or an observer to, this type of "crèche mess," you can help save the day for your town by promoting a compromise that all parties will find satisfactory.

The thing to remember is that neither side is completely right, yet neither is completely wrong. The display advocates are right when they insist that people should be allowed to express their beliefs. The civil libertarians are correct when they insist that such expressions should not impinge on the rights of others. If both sides agree that these principal points are well-taken, a solution may be at hand.

For example, if it's feared that a holiday display on public property could be misinterpreted as government endorsement of a certain belief set, the scene could be staged on private property. Many merchants and landowners would be delighted to serve as host for the display. If City Hall is the only available central location for the holiday scene, it can be an ecumenical tribute to the spirit of the season rather than a religious statement. If you start with the theme "peace on Earth," you can develop a creative holiday representation that everyone in town will embrace eagerly.

Step up as the peacemaker before positions become entrenched. You'll be providing your community with an object lesson in brotherhood. We all could use the occasional refresher course on that subject.

90.

The Primacy of
Family and Friends

People around the world celebrate holidays with a rich and compelling diversity of traditions. Consider how Christmas—just one holiday—is observed in different nations around the world.

In the United States and Canada, of course, we're used to the image of Santa Claus, decked in red, delivering toys to children with the aid of his reindeer. In Russia, however, the Santa figure is known as Grandfather Frost, and he wears blue rather than red.

In Denmark, Santa's sleigh is pulled by reindeer, but in Belgium, horses power the jolly old elf's sleigh. In Spain, it also is believed that horses do the heavy work—but not for Santa. Instead, they bear the wise men, who each year reenact their journey to Bethlehem. It's one of that trio, Balthazar, who dispenses gifts to children. You might expect reindeer to be the principal transport mode in Sweden. They're not. Swedish youngsters imagine Santa's chauffeur as a goat.

We in the U.S. think of Santa's base as the North Pole; in other lands, he resides much closer to home, or even in the home itself. The Swedish people envision Santa, or *tomte*, as he's known, emerging from the floor of their houses or barns. Danish children learn that Santa's elves live in the attics of their homes; they feed these little helpers rice pudding and saucers of milk rather than cookies and glasses of milk.

Even our tradition of exchanging gifts on Christmas Day has some interesting twists internationally. Italians, for example, exchange gifts on January 6, the day that many believe the wise men finally reached the baby Jesus. In France, children open their gifts on Christmas, but adults typically wait until New Year's Day.

Breathtaking as the range of Christmas traditions may be, observances in most nations are based on the primacy of family and friends. No matter how customs may diverge, celebrations most often center on a large, festive meal that brings loved ones together in appreciation of each other's company. The nations of the world are telling us that friends and family are the most important feature of holidays—if we didn't know that already.

91.

Making the Key
Holiday Decisions

Holiday celebrations include many elements, such as hosting, cooking, decorating, entertainment, gifts, and travel. While the importance of each of these components varies from holiday to holiday, it seems reasonable to conclude that successful holidays are those that are well-coordinated.

On many occasions, though, our affairs are less than that; they may even be haphazard. This can occur when no one steps up to the plate to assume the job of holiday manager, or because more than one person in the family covets the job. Perhaps you would like to plan the holiday for your family, yet you avoid saying so, lest your request be misinterpreted as unseemly. Maybe you sense that your sister would like the job, so you back away rather than risk dissension. However, if your sister demurs for the same reason, then your holiday may be catch as catch can, a scenario likely to please no one.

Holidays *require* coordination, so one of the first jobs of your family should be to designate a manager. Many families pick managers based on tradition. Mom and Dad always have managed holidays, so everyone assumes that they'll continue in that role. Yet it's entirely possible that Mom and Dad, eager for a break from responsibility, would like to pass the baton to someone else. They won't initiate the change, though, for fear of upsetting family harmony.

Clearly, what's needed is a family discussion—well in advance of the holiday involved—to flesh out all of the issues that often are difficult for families to articulate. The meeting of the minds will give everyone a sense of who wants overall planning responsibilities, who can help the manager, and who won't be able to do much but show up on time. Once roles are assigned, all family members will know exactly what's expected of them, and all are likely to do an excellent job, as a result.

With the team and responsibilities delineated, your holiday affair will be a smashing success—but don't assume that all roles will remain the same for the next holiday. Circumstances change, so the assignments of your family members will change, as well. Keep bringing the team together for those all-important discussions.

92.

Design the Holiday
That You Want

To have a successful holiday, you first must know what you want from that holiday. That may seem simplistic, but consider: How many times have holidays descended on you when you weren't ready for them or hadn't discussed them with your family? How many times did your loved ones assume that you would be celebrating as you had in previous years without offering or soliciting input regarding this year's affair? When that occurred, were you pleased with the results?

Holidays that simply "happen" without any advance planning may not happen for the best, but you can take charge of the situation by designing the holiday that you want. To illustrate, let's look at a hypothetical Independence Day, a warm-weather holiday that offers many options for celebration. You may have a half-formed vision of a family picnic at a lush local park, but if you don't share your idea with your loved ones soon enough, you may find that every grove in the park already is reserved, and you'll be hosting a backyard barbecue once more.

Perhaps you'd like to get away over Independence Day. If you wait too long to detail your trip, you may find that flights—as well as hotels in your destination city—are completely booked, not an unusual occurrence for important holidays. It's back to the barbecue once more.

In another case, maybe you've been working so hard that you're looking forward to nothing more taxing than a languorous long weekend—no family, no barbecue, just a recliner, a cool drink, and maybe a ballgame or two on the tube. If you announce your plans too late, you may throw your family into a tizzy, since they were looking forward to the traditional barbecue and now have no fallback.

What's clear from these examples is that to simultaneously keep peace in the family and achieve the holiday that you want, you must solidify and articulate your goals—early and often. Your relatives then can accommodate your wishes in their own planning. If you spring a major change on them without sufficient notice—"No barbecue this year, folks"—it may be you who ends up skewered.

93.

When Compromise Is Necessary

As an efficient planner and manager, you have firm ideas on just about every aspect of holidays. You know when you want the festivities to begin, what foods should be prepared, what entertainment should be on the agenda, and who will be responsible for each task associated with the celebration. Ordinarily, your family is thrilled to have you as their holiday CEO—largely because it frees them up for holidays of pure pleasure unencumbered by heavy duties.

However, you may encounter holidays where your plans clash with those of other family members. You may favor an early start to the affair so that you can conclude at a reasonable hour and have sufficient time for cleanup—and for making the mental transition back to work mode. Some of your relatives, however, may need a later start to the party so that they can attend their in-laws' celebrations early in the day. In another example, you're the traditional host and confidently expect the family to arrive en masse at your home, as usual. However, relatives who can't travel this particular year inform you that they would like the family to gather at their house; if they can't host, they can't attend.

This unexpected clash of needs may bring your blood to the boiling point. After all, you may reason, you've been managing these affairs for years. Couldn't they at least show some respect for, and deference to, your wishes?

While this reaction is understandable, it's not one that's likely to yield the most harmonious holiday. Deal with these situations calmly. Think again about your most important objectives for holidays—to bring your family together and celebrate as a unit. Sometimes, achieving that overriding goal means compromise on one or more less vital elements.

When compromise is called for, do it cheerily. If circumstances mean that you won't be hosting, offer to help the new host in any way possible. If a later start to your celebration becomes necessary, find an effective way to use those few hours early in the day that have been returned to you. You'll never get everything you want with a compromise, but if it keeps the family together and happy, you'll get what you want most.

94.

When Little Things Go Wrong

Holidays are complex. We envision them as treasured moments of peace and love when we're buffered by family and friends from the frustrations of the everyday world. They can be exactly that, but getting there means a lot of hard work and the coordination of many moving parts. Inevitably, not all of those parts will mesh smoothly, despite your best efforts.

Little things will go wrong. A flight delay keeps Gram and Gramps from arriving on time. Fluffy, your cat, knocks an heirloom ornament from the tree and uses it as a soccer ball. No one seems interested in that fantastic new dessert that you created from scratch. It rains on your Independence Day picnic.

Ordinarily, we would take these little hiccups in stride, treating them with humor and understanding, but the holidays may leave us so edgy and tense that even tiny glitches such as these can threaten to send us into full-blown hysteria. You *can* keep the proper perspective on holiday gaffes. If you develop and implement a holiday plan, you'll be confident that all the big items will be taken care of just as you envision them. If you're comfortable with your plan, you'll be able to accommodate smallish deviations—and even devise some creative alternatives to work around the problems.

Since you know that you're achieving your most important objectives, you can live with—and even laugh at—the little things that go wrong. Misadventures even can become part of your cherished holiday memories.

When you think back to the year that Aunt Edna broke a dish from your favorite holiday china, you'll recall it warmly—because it reminds you of the joy that you shared with your family and friends that day. Peculiar as it seems, the little things that go wrong can remind us of the important things that go right.

95.

Factor In Some Spontaneity

If your uncle announces that he's taking the kids out to see the displays of lights in the neighborhood, do you nix the trip because you fear that they won't be back to open presents at the time your family always opens presents? If this sounds like you, you may be squeezing too much spontaneity from your holiday celebrations.

"Planned spontaneity" means that you should allow for some spur-of-the-moment playfulness when you're organizing your event. Remember that you as the holiday manager have a much greater need than other family members to stick to the game plan, which is largely your creation. Your loved ones may be thinking more of fun than orderliness when they envision the holiday.

When you build spontaneity into your plan, you allow others to shape their own affairs. Your family is more likely to agree to the holiday that you plan when you entertain their suggestions, so when they offer them, modify them as common sense dictates and then—do nothing. There's nothing that you need to do, as spontaneity is now part of your plan.

96.

Bad Weather—
The Uninvited Guest

If you're serious about holidays, you plan them down to the most minute detail. The one thing that you can't account for is bad weather. It's like a wayward relative who crashes the party. You didn't invite this black cloud to hover over your affair, but there it is—what can you do about it?

When we think of weather and its impact on holidays, we tend to focus on the havoc that ice, snow, and wind can wreak on the winter holidays in the Northeast and Midwest. However, other regions—and other holidays—hardly are immune. Many a Labor Day, for example, is played out against hurricane warnings—sometimes even actual hurricanes—all along the Atlantic and Gulf coasts. Rain is a threat to Halloween trick-or-treating and Independence Day and Memorial Day picnics everywhere.

We don't want something as capricious as weather to interrupt our holidays, so we may doggedly pursue our plans, even at the expense of personal safety. We drive on icy highways to get to

Grandma's house, or we stubbornly sit in our picnic groves, oblivious to the driving rain and flashes of lightning.

If this sounds like you, you need to rethink your heroism. One thing that is paramount is the well-being of you, your family, and your friends. That always should be your top priority. Instead of trying to ignore hazardous conditions, work on developing an understanding that weather is an unpredictable element that every so often will affect your holidays. Get comfortable with that notion now, and you'll be less angry—and less determined to endanger yourself—when foul weather strikes.

Once you reach a comfort zone regarding weather, you'll be better prepared to approach the matter as the pragmatic planner that you usually are. You'll be prepared, for instance, to develop weather-inspired backup plans, such as shifting your outdoor bash to a suitable indoor location, or calling a halt to all travel until the roads are safe again. Implementation of alternate plans requires significant coordination and frequent communication among everyone associated with the celebration—but you're well-equipped for that role. You've demonstrated your skills in holiday management time and again.

97.

An Out-of-Body Experience

Most holiday planners are so dedicated to the task that they remember to include every detail save one—their own expectations and wishes. Often, if you forget to factor in your own needs, you end up not getting exactly the holiday that you want, leaving you feeling unappreciated and resentful—and perhaps looking for someone to blame. That's not at all the result that you had in mind.

You can avoid this by casting yourself in two roles. You're the coordinator of the holiday, of course, but you're also a valued participant. As you go through your preparations, always consider both functions. This is a way of ensuring that your needs are addressed.

For example, you typically commit a lot of time to the holiday meal, fashioning a menu that will please everyone, selecting the best ingredients, and worrying about which china to use and the most agreeable seating arrangement. Yet here's a question you may never have considered—what would *you* like to eat as part of the holiday repast? Once you determine the answer, you the manager should include this dish for you the participant.

The timing of the event is yet another area where your needs should count. Some family members may prefer an early beginning so that they can travel home before darkness falls. Others traditionally favor a later start so that they can sleep in or perhaps enjoy early afternoon football games before dinner. What schedule works best for you? It's perfectly reasonable to ask that question—and just as reasonable to incorporate the answer into your plans.

This is not to suggest that you arbitrarily impose your will on the gathering. That would be just as wrongheaded as ignoring your needs. Instead, articulate your wishes to the family. Let them know what you want, and encourage them to share their needs with you. With active dialogue, you'll usually find a way to satisfy most needs of most loved ones—including you. That will result in a happy holiday for both of you—the planner and the participant.

98.

A Movable Feast

Holidays provide us with a comfort zone. Each year, we celebrate certain holidays in a big way while barely observing others. It's the way that we do it, the way that we've always done it, the way with which we're most comfortable. The very notion of changes in our pattern of holidays may be unsettling to us, yet holidays are something of a movable feast.

For example, you may think of Mother's Day and Father's Day as two of the anchors of your life, yet for most of American history, these were not recognized formally as holidays. Mother's Day was not an official national holiday until it was so proclaimed by President Woodrow Wilson in 1914. Father's Day began informally in Spokane, Washington in 1910, and though we've celebrated it throughout our lives, it wasn't formally designated as an official national holiday— tied to a certain day each year—until President Lyndon Johnson decreed it so in 1966. That same year, 1966, brought the creation of Kwanzaa, a new holiday that has grown in importance and impact since then.

Even in cases when holidays have been around for centuries, their meaning may have changed over the years. Take Halloween, a holiday with both Celtic and Christian roots. The Celts not only used Halloween to mark the final harvest of the year, but they also believed that this changing of the seasons brought the spirits of the dead close to the living. One can only imagine what the Celts would think if they saw their serious beliefs represented by our own irreverent Halloween decor of tombstones, spider webs, and witches on brooms.

The point is not that the Celts were right and we're wrong. Rather, it's that beliefs and cultural norms are subject to change, so it's only natural that the holidays that reflect society's beliefs and norms change, as well. We can resist new or evolving holidays if we choose, but it's so much more satisfying to study them, understand them, and observe them if it seems appropriate.

So if you're invited to take part in a Kwanzaa celebration but hold back because you disapprove of new holidays, take the plunge. Don't think of your holiday comfort zone as being invaded. Think of it as being expanded.

99.

To a Multicultural Celebration

See if this sounds familiar: Your kids come home from school with excited but worried looks on their faces. They explain that their teachers asked the pupils to sing some holiday songs, even though your children don't observe the holiday involved. So now, your kids want to know what they should do. Of course, you always intended to formally steep your children in faith and values, but it's a little earlier for that than you had planned. Nevertheless, the problem is before you, so you must act.

A good first step is to realize that classroom singing is an innocent, joyous act. It is not war by other means. Neither nations nor religions will rise or fall on the songs that ring from local classrooms. In some schools, teachers, administrators, and parents get so emotionally involved in this issue that their positions calcify, making creative solutions that much more difficult to find.

If you're calm but purposeful, you're ready for the next step— contacting the school to determine what their approach to holiday observation actually is, since your kids might have distorted it just a bit. Where you can, schedule a personal meeting with the principal or other high-ranking official. If that's not possible, a phone conversation can work, too.

Should the principal outline a program that includes all faiths and cultures, you have the assurance that you need—but if the program comes up short on the diversity scale, you might suggest some ideas for improvement. Better still, volunteer to work with the school and other parents to implement a holiday celebration that promotes diversity.

It's very likely that your suggestions and offer of help will be warmly received. However, should you encounter indifference or resistance, remember that principals must be responsive to school boards, school district officials, and parent-teacher organizations. Any of these can be a vehicle for your ideas about diversity in your kids' school.

Once you're certain that the school's observances are appropriate, you're ready to explain to your kids that they can participate in all aspects of the celebration, since it's so inclusive. They'll be showing respect for others' beliefs, even as others display similar regard for your family's beliefs. You'll enable your children to enjoy the school's multicultural holiday—and teach them a valuable lesson in the process.

100.

The Ideal Holiday

What, after all, constitutes the ideal holiday? Participants will measure the success of holidays in different ways, depending on the goals that they establish for the occasions. Some will consider the holiday a great triumph if they receive all of the gifts on their wish lists—a regrettably narrow outlook. Others, still focusing on gifts, will be thrilled if the presents that they offer are well-received. Still others regard winning holidays as those where the entire family shares a day of harmony without reviving long-dormant quarrels.

While there may be no universal way of evaluating our holiday affairs, it can help to remember that most of these special occasions were created to remember heroes, leaders, and noble ideals. In some cases, we've strayed from the original purpose of holidays—however unintentionally—in favor of events that are largely social in nature.

Social gatherings are great—think of them as the "micro" element of holidays, that which addresses personal needs. However, there's also the "macro" component, which might be thought of as

attention to the aims and themes of the holiday. The most memorable holidays blend micro and macro features.

For example, if you assemble your family for Thanksgiving dinner, you've done well on the micro side. Getting everybody together in the same place, on the same day, can be quite a feat. If you also encourage your loved ones to spend a moment appreciating the bounty that they enjoy, you register on the macro meter, as well.

If you stage a wonderful Independence Day picnic that offers great food and lively entertainment, that's a micro success. If you conduct the picnic on a site of importance in America's development and accompany your kids to the local historical museum, you also score a macro coup.

Of course, not every holiday will lend itself to this dual focus. At times, you'll be too busy or distracted for the complicated planning that may be required. However, when the opportunity is there, go for it. Shoot for success on the micro and macro fronts. When it all comes together, you'll have the ideal holiday.